BASIC TRAINING
for trainers

A handbook
for new trainers

GARY KROEHNERT

McGRAW-HILL BOOK COMPANY Sydney
New York   San Francisco   Auckland   Bogotá
Caracas   Lisbon   London   Madrid   Mexico City
Milan   Montreal   New Delhi   San Juan
Singapore   Tokyo   Toronto

First published 1990
Reprinted 1992, 1993 (twice) 1994

Revised edition 1995
Reprinted 1995

A52703

National Library of Australia
Cataloguing-in-Publication data:

Kroehnert, Gary.
Basic training for trainers.

Rev. ed.
Bibliography.
Includes index.
ISBN 0 07 470193 2.

1. Employees-Training of. 1. Title.

658.312404

Produced in Australia by McGraw-Hill Book Company Australia Pty Limited
4 Barcoo Street Roseville, NSW 2069
Typeset in Australia by Craftsmen Type & Art
Printed in Australia by Star Printery Pty. Limited

Publisher:	John Rowe
Acquisitions Editor:	Craig Bouma
Production Editor:	Kirsten Lees
Designer:	Robin Board
Cartoonist:	Yolande Bull and Robin Board
Technical Illustrator:	Alistair Barnard

Contents

Preface

In the first edition of *Basic Training* I said that in many ways the design, presentation and evaluation of a course is like the preparation of a meal. A meal is not simply the collection of various foods which are thrown into a pot to cook. The ingredients have to be selected according to the recipe, they have to be prepared, and they have to be cooked individually, perhaps using different methods and having other ingredients added to them in the correct sequence while they are cooking.

If the various elements are collected, prepared and organized properly we will have a professional looking presentation. If the presentation looks good, we have the best chance of it being taken without resistance. If the course is taken, enjoyed and sustains life or develops growth, isn't it possible that we have taken care of the evaluation as well? I have not changed my thoughts on this; in fact they have been really reinforced over the past few years.

This second edition still has all the same ingredients as the first edition (some of them slightly modified), but it has two additional ingredients included to suit new tastes. They are 'competency based training' and 'outdoor based training'. These two additional ingredients have been included because of their topical nature these days, or as they sometimes seem to be the flavours of the year (pun intended).

Modifications include the new enlarged format. This new edition has been specifically designed to allow you plenty of space to make notes and observations on the pages as you go. The many forms have also been enlarged so that you can make full use of them.

As with the first edition of *Basic Training* it is not intended that this book be a complete resource in itself. It is again intended that this book be written in simple, easy-to-understand terms. It should become part of a simple resource kit for the trainer or student. It is meant to give the new trainer an overview of the main competencies in which they will need to develop skills.

Most chapters have their own application example and a list of resources for further reading. I have not included texts which were found to be too awkward for the newcomer. If you would like to suggest other inclusions please fill in the form found at the back of this text with your suggestions. This form may also be used for comments on layout, spelling, or anything you wish. These suggestions will be evaluated for inclusion in further editions.

After you have read this text, it is hoped that it will be kept as a quick reference guide. Perhaps some of the checklists may be reused by the reader.

Gary Kroehnert

> *Educators need the ability to accept the things they can't change, the courage to change the things they can change, and the cunning to recognise the difference.*

CHAPTER 1

The principles of adult learning

The term 'learning' has many interpretations, but is generally accepted as a change in behavior or attitude. It's not intended that in this chapter we analyse the theories behind adult learning, but it is intended to put forward some of the accepted principles of adult learning. These principles listed here are basically the same as put forward in any 'methods instruction' course; the only difference is that the principles will vary in name.

These principles deal with training and education, and are common to the formal classroom setting as well as on-the-job training. Any form of training should include as many of these nine principles as possible.

We can easily remember the nine principles of learning by using the mnemonic RAMP 2 FAME.

R   Recency
A   Appropriateness
M   Motivation
P   Primacy
2   2-way communication
F   Feedback
A   Active learning
M   Multi-sense learning
E   Exercise

Nine principles

These principles are important in several ways. They allow you to prepare a session properly, to present the session efficiently and effectively and they also allow you to evaluate the session.

We will now look at the ideas behind these terms. It's important to note that these are not presented in a priority order; they all deserve equal consideration.

R: Recency

The law of Recency tells us that the things that are learned last are those best remembered by the participant. This applies in two separate areas of learning. Firstly, it applies to the content at the end of the session and, secondly, it applies to the things that are freshest in the participants' minds. For the first application, it's important for the trainer to summarize frequently and to ensure that the key messages are emphasized again at the end of the session. For the second application, it indicates that trainers should plan review sections into their presentations.

Factors to consider about Recency are:

- Keep each session to a relatively short period of time, no longer than twenty minutes if possible.
- If sessions are longer than twenty minutes, recap often. This breaks the larger sessions into smaller sessions with lots of endings so that you can summarise.
- The end of every session is important. Recap the whole session, highlighting the key points or key messages.
- Keep the participants fully aware of the direction and progress of their learning.

A: Appropriateness

The law of Appropriateness says that all the training, information, training aids, case studies and other materials must be appropriate to the participants' needs. They can easily lose motivation if the trainer fails to keep the materials relevant to their needs. In addition, trainers must continually let participants know how the new information links with previous knowledge, so that we remove their fears of the unknown.

Factors to consider about Appropriateness:

- The trainer should clearly identify a need for the participants to be taking part in the training. With this need identified, the trainer must make sure that everything connected with the session is appropriate to that need.
- Use descriptions, examples or illustrations that the participants are familiar with.

M: Motivation

The law of Motivation shows us that the participants must want to learn, they must be ready to learn and there must be some reason to learn. Trainers find that if participants have strong motivation to learn, or a sense of purpose, they will excel in their learning. Once motivation has been created the learning atmosphere opens up. If we fail to use the law of Appropriateness and neglect to make the materials relevant, we will almost certainly lose participants' motivation.

Factors to consider about Motivation are:

- The material must be meaningful and worthwhile to the participant, not only to the trainer.
- Not only must the participants be motivated, so must the trainer. If the trainer isn't motivated, learning probably won't take place.
- As mentioned in the law of Appropriateness the trainer sometimes needs to identify a need for the participants to be there. Trainers can usually create motivation by telling the participants that this session can fill that need.
- Move from the known to the unknown. Start the session at a point the participants are familiar with. Gradually build up and link points together so that everyone knows where they are expected to go in the learning process.

P: Primacy

The law of Primacy states that the things participants learn first are usually learnt best so the first impressions or pieces of information that participants get from the trainer are really important. For this reason it's good practice to include all of the key points at the beginning of the session. During the session expand on the key points, and other associated information. Also to be included with the law of Primacy is the fact that when participants are shown how to do something they must be shown the correct way the first time. The reason for this is that it's sometimes very difficult to 'unteach' a participant if they get things wrong the first time.

Factors to consider about Primacy are:

- Again keep sessions to a relatively short period of time; twenty minutes is about right as suggested with the law of Recency.
- The beginning of your session will be important as you know that most of the participants will be listening; so make it interesting and put lots of important information into it.
- Keep the participants fully aware of the direction and progress of their learning.
- Ensure that participants get things right the first time you require them to do something.

2: 2-way communication

The law of 2-way communication quite clearly states that the training process involves communication *with* the participants, not *at* them. Any form of presentation should be a 2-way communication. This doesn't necessarily mean that the whole session should be a discussion, but it must allow for interaction between the trainer/facilitator and the trainee/ participant.

Factors to consider about 2-way communication are:

- Your body language is also included in 2-way communication: make sure it matches what you're saying.
- Your session plan should have interactions with the participants designed into it.

F: Feedback

The law of Feedback informs us that both the facilitator and the participant need information from each other. The facilitator needs to know that the participants are following and keeping pace and the participants need feedback on the standard of their performance.

Reinforcement is also required with feedback. If we reward participants (positive reinforcement) for doing things right, we have a far greater chance of getting them to change their behavior to a desired outcome. Be aware, though, that too many negative reinforcements may not have the final response required.

Factors to consider about Feedback are:

- Trainees should be tested frequently for instructor feedback.
- When trainees are tested they must get feedback on their performance as soon as possible.
- Testing can also include the trainer asking frequent questions of the group.
- All feedback doesn't have to be positive, as some people believe. Positive feedback is only half of it, and is almost useless without negative feedback.
- When a participant does or says something right, acknowledge it (in front of the group if possible).
- Prepare your presentations so that there is positive reinforcement built into it at the very beginning.
- Look for someone doing it right as well as always looking for someone doing it wrong.

A: Active learning

The law of Active learning shows us that participants learn more when they are actively involved in the process. Remember the saying 'we learn by doing'? This is important in the training of adults. If you want to instruct a group in writing reports, don't just tell them how it should be done; get them to do it. Another benefit of this is that adults are generally not used to sitting in a classroom setting all day, so the use of active learning will assist you in keeping them awake.

Factors to consider about Active learning are:

- Use practical exercises during the instruction.
- Use plenty of questions during the instruction.
- A quick quiz may be used to keep the participants active.
- If at all possible get the participants to do what they are being instructed in.
- If the participants are kept sitting for long periods without any participation or questions being asked of them it's possible for them to nod off or lose interest in the session.

M: Multiple-sense learning

The law of Multiple-sense learning says that learning is far more effective if the participants use more than one of their five senses. If you tell trainees about a new type of sandwich filling they may remember it. If you show them the product they probably will remember it. If you let them touch, smell and taste it as well, there is no way they will forget about it.

Avoid the dangers of boredom by keeping your group alert with Multiple-sense learning

Factors to consider about Multiple-sense learning are:
- If you tell participants about something, try to show them as well.
- Use as many of the participants' senses as necessary for them to learn, but don't get carried away.
- When using Multiple-sense learning make sure that the sense selected can be used. Ensure that it's not difficult for the group to hear, see and touch whatever it is you want them to.

I hear and I forget,
I see and I remember,
I do and I understand.
Confucius c. 450 BC

E: Exercise

The law of Exercise indicates that things that are repeated are best remembered. By getting participants to exercise or repeat new information we are increasing the possibility of them being able to recall that information at a later time. Multiplication tables learnt at school are one example of exercise. It's best if the trainer can encourage exercise, or overlearning, by repeating information in different ways. Perhaps the trainer could talk about the new process or item, then show an overhead or diagram, show the finished product and finally get the participants to carry out the required task several times. Exercise also includes intensity. The law of exercise is also referred to as overlearning or meaningful repetition.

Factors to consider about Exercise are:
- The more we get trainees to repeat something the more likely they are to retain the information.
- By asking frequent questions we are encouraging exercise or overlearning.
- The participants must perform the exercise themselves; but taking notes doesn't count.
- Summarize frequently as this is another form of exercise. Always summarize at the conclusion of a session.
- Get the participants to recall frequently what has been covered so far in the presentation.
- The law of Exercise also includes giving participants exercises to carry out.

It's often stated that without some form of exercise, participants will forget one quarter of what they have learnt within six hours, one-third within twenty-four hours and around ninety per cent within six weeks.

Conclusion

These principles of learning relate to training and education. They are used in all areas whether in a classroom setting or on-the-job. They can be used with children and adolescents as well as adults. Effective instruction should use as many of these principles as possible, if not all of them. When you plan a session, look through the draft to make sure that these principles have been used and if they haven't, maybe a revision is in order.

Application example

To give an effective instruction in applying arm slings (using the principles of learning), it was decided to use the following format:

- Motivational introduction, to include objectives and overview of the session.
- Link back to previous sessions.
- Tell participants how it is done.
- Show participants how it is done.
- Get participants to repeat (under control).
- Participants to practise on each other.
- Praise good work done by participants.
- Evaluation (testing of objectives).
- Summarize at end of session.
- Emphasize the key points.
- Link forward to next session.

Looking at the above we can see that the nine principles of adult learning have been used.

Further reading

Baird, L., Schneier, C. & Laird, D., *The Training and Development Sourcebook*, Human Resource Press, Massachusetts, 1985, Section IV.

Dowling, J. R. & Drolet, R. P., *Developing and Administering an Industrial Training Program*, CBI Publishing, Massachusetts, 1979, Part 1.

Goad, Tom, *Delivering Effective Training*, University Associates, California, 1982, Chapter 3.

Goldstein, Irwin, *Training: Program Development and Evaluation*, Brooks/Cole Publishing, California, 1974, Chapters 6 & 7.

Recency	We have used recency a number of times during the session by breaking the larger session down into a number of smaller sessions.
Appropriateness	We have made the material appropriate to the participants at the beginning of the session.
Motivation	We have given the group reasons to be here and to listen to us, it has been made relevant to them.
Primacy	We have used the primacy effect a number of times during the session the same way we did with recency. We have broken the session up to give us lots of 'ends'. Note that the total session uses primacy and recency as well by using a properly structured beginning and conclusion.
2-way communication	We have allowed for, and encouraged, communication between the trainer and the participants. It has been designed into the session.
Feedback	We have allowed for feedback during the whole session. Positive reinforcement has also been designed into the beginning of the session to encourage participation.
Active learning	Both the trainer and the participants are constantly moving around and doing things.
Multi-sense learning	We have included multi-sense learning by using hearing, sight and touch.
Exercise	This has been exercised by getting the participants to not only listen, but also to watch, do and practise.

Laird, Dugan, *Approaches to Training and Development*, Addison-Wesley Publishing Company, Massachusetts, 1978, Chapter 9.

Rogers, Jennifer, *Adults Learning*, 2nd edn, Open University Press, England, 1979, Chapters 1, 2 & 3.

CHAPTER 2

Training needs analysis

This is a term being used more and more each day but unfortunately many people do not fully understand its meaning. So, what is a 'training needs analysis'? To answer this question we first need to understand what is meant by a 'training need'. A training need exists when there is a gap between what is required of a person to perform their duties competently and what they actually know that enables them to do so. A training needs analysis is the method of determining if a training need exists and if it does, what training is required to fill the gap.

Generally, the training needs analysis will highlight the subject matter needing to be covered during the instruction. The knowledge gained by the participants will help to increase their level of ability and allow them to perform their tasks at an acceptable level.

An example of this situation may be where a company purchases a number of new computers. The company has not used computers before and none of the staff have any experience with them. This is a very simple example of a training need. The training needs analysis in this case is simply a matter of noting such an obvious need.

Using the above example let us now say that the company did have some computers before, but a different type, and that some of the staff had

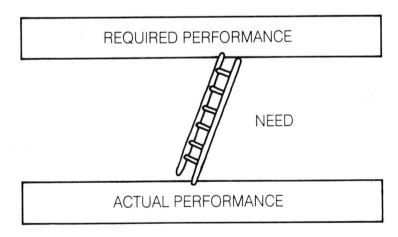

A training needs analysis identifies the gap between required performance and actual performance

some experience with them. In this situation we can again see a training need, but the solution is not as obvious. By carrying out a training needs analysis we would be able to target the group to be trained and also find out what training was required.

Needs can be identified in any number of areas and some of the more common ways for them to be identified are:

- complaints from staff
- complaints from customers/clients
- poor quality of work
- frequent errors
- overhandling items
- inadequate recruiting process
- large staff turnover
- performance dates not met
- conflicts among staff
- new equipment/systems.

This list is not comprehensive and each organization may have different indicators to show a training need. The important thing is that once a training need or gap has been identified, it should be filled.

When we carry out a training needs analysis we are usually interested in collecting the following types of information:

- job roles
- job process
- task list
- job problems
- task frequency
- task difficulty
- task importance.

motivate him to do it.

A simple statement that should be applied to any identified performance problem is, 'If a person's life depended on them performing a skill and they could do it, it's a management problem. If they couldn't do it, it's a training problem.' Management problems cannot always be solved by training and may need to be handed back to management to solve.

Conducting a training needs analysis

Carrying out a training needs analysis is largely a matter of getting information from people. How this information is gathered is up to the person carrying out the survey. They also need to consider the cost and time restrictions. It is generally accepted that a training needs analysis is instigated by management when a problem becomes noticeable, although a competent training department may notice the same thing.

We can use as a simple example a request from management that a problem be fixed. We would firstly interview management to find out the exact nature of the problem. At the same time we should make sure that it is a training problem and not something else, like obsolete equipment. After the details have been gathered we need to check with the people doing the work where the problem is to make sure that they do have a training need. If they can perform the task required, without training, it is not a training problem and so should be referred to management. To establish a training need we must identify that there is a gap in knowledge, skills or attitudes.

Management may be the first to notice that a performance problem exists

Other items that may be able to assist us in our training needs analysis are:

- accident reports
- company plan, policy or projections
- exit interviews
- legislation
- error rates
- complaints

- absenteeism
- quality control reports
- market research reports
- performance appraisals
- observation
- testing
- job analysis.

These items could contain important information for us. As a single document it may tell us that the factory has a 17 per cent rejection rate on standard components. As a combined source of information it may tell us that the factory has a 17 per cent rejection rate on standard components, a 32 per cent turnover of staff per annum and 34 per cent of the workers are over-qualified for their positions. This information would add greatly to the information gained through surveys or interviews with the management and staff.

Another common method used in planning the contents of a training course is the questionnaire. A well-designed questionnaire can be used for all levels of employee. On the next page is a sample questionnaire that has been designed to gain information on subjects for a first line supervisors course; it is typical of the questionnaires used to collect course content information.

Once the information from all sources has been gathered, it must be processed. The results are looked at closely to ensure that training is the appropriate answer to the problem. When it has been agreed that training is in order, we again use the training needs analysis to prepare the training.

The chain may look like the diagram on page 14.

When the need has been established, it is relatively easy to determine a general course content and we may refine it with assistance from the management and participants. Then specific learning objectives should be written and they lead us to our detailed course content. With this specific information, the trainer designs suitable instruction to give participants the appropriate knowledge, skills or attitudes required to perform the task or duty to the level required.

Note that with this sequence we are increasing the cost in dollars to the company and the amount of our time involvement. Something that should always be considered is whether the cost of training may be more costly than living with the problem. In such a case it would be acceptable to leave the situation unchanged, unless directed to continue for either internal or external political reasons.

Please tick any topic you feel is relevant to our supervisor training	strong need	some need	little need
Principles of supervision			
The role of the supervisor			
Induction of new employees			
Training of new employees			
Training of existing employees			
Appraisal of staff			
Principles of communication			
Oral communication			
Written communication			
Equal employment opportunities			
Listening skills			
Counselling skills			
Interviewing skills			
Disciplining skills			
Handling meetings			
Time management			
Delegation skills			
Financial control			
Health and safety			
Stress management skills			
Multicultural skills			
Computers			
Handling complaints and grievances			
Handling difficult clients			
Staff selection skills			
Initiating change			
Career development			

Please fill in the following information and return to _____ by the end of this month. (This information is strictly confidential and will only be used to assess training needs.)

Name: _____

Position: _____

Location: _____

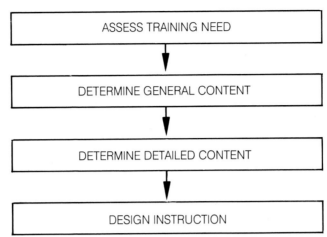

Once a training need has been identified, the trainer can develop suitable instruction

Conclusion

We have seen that the procedure for designing and conducting a training needs analysis need not be complicated. It is a logical process and simply needs a common-sense approach. Those involved in the process must be prepared to devote a significant amount of time to it. The cost of such an analysis could be quite high and this needs to be considered from the outset.

We may also use the training needs analysis to assist us in determining the level of instruction. The analysis can show details such as the age, educational standard, social level and sex of our trainees.

One of the obvious problems that a lot of trainers see is the evaluation of the training. After the training needs analysis has been carried out and training has taken place, the process may appear to have been completed; but evaluation is often neglected. After training has taken place we should carry out some form of evaluation. We need to find out whether the training objectives have been met, whether the original problem has been rectified by the training and whether the training program could be improved. (See Chapter 12 which has information on evaluation.)

Application example

A reasonably large courier company (54 employees) had identified a number of problems with their organization. Some of the problems included lost and damaged parcels, a high turnover of staff, numerous vehicle breakdowns, a growing number of customer complaints and branches not meeting their sales budgets.

The company decided to call in a specialist to tackle the problem. The consultant was requested to carry out a training needs analysis.

The steps taken by the consultant were to:

- become familiar with the structure of the company
- become familiar with the finances of the company
- become familiar with the staff in the company
- design a suitable questionnaire to establish a training need
- follow up the questionnaire with personal interviews
- establish whether the needs shown were training needs or management problems
- decide whether to train or leave things be
- design training to fill the gap indicated
- conduct training
- evaluate training by observing behavioral and attitudinal changes
- evaluate training by comparing the problems identified now with the problems identified before training
- modify or revise the training course if necessary.

It can be seen in this example that the whole process is ongoing. Modification or revision to a course is usually necessary each time something changes within the organization. If a course is not modified to suit changes, problems could be expected to arise at a future date. It is much easier, and cheaper, to fix things before they happen rather than after; prevention is far better than cure.

Further reading

Baird, L., Schneier, C. & Laird, D., *The Training and Development Sourcebook*, Human Resource Press, Massachusetts, 1985, Section II.

Boydell, T. H., *A Guide to the Identification of Training Needs*, 2nd edn, British Association for Commercial and Industrial Education, London, 1983.

Craig, Robert, *Training and Development Handbook*, 2nd edn, McGraw-Hill Book Company, New York, 1976, Chapter 9.

Dowling, J. R. & Drolet, R. P., *Developing and Administering an Industrial Training Program*, CBI Publishing, Massachusetts, 1979.

Goldstein, Irwin, *Training: Program Development and Evaluation*, Brooks/Cole Publishing, California, 1974, Chapters 2 & 3.

Laird, Dugan, *Approaches to Training and Development*, Addison-Wesley Publishing Company, Massachusetts, 1978, Chapter 5.

Pennington, F. C., *Assessing Educational Needs of Adults*, New Directions for Continuing Education Quarterly Sourcebooks, Jossey-Bass, San Francisco, 1980, Series No. 7.

Zemke, R. & Kramlinger, T., *Figuring Things Out: A Trainer's Guide to Needs and Task Analysis*, Addison-Wesley Publishing Company, Massachusetts, 1981, Chapter 14.

CHAPTER 3

Survey methods and techniques

We will be dealing with three basic survey methods in this chapter. The three methods to be discussed are: personal interviews, mail questionnaires and telephone interviews.

What is a survey?

A survey in this sense is the process of gathering information to determine whether or not there is a training need. There are other types of surveys but they are generally not of interest to the trainer.

What is a survey used for?

Surveys are normally used to identify training gaps and to provide a training needs analysis. If a survey is conducted satisfactorily it makes our job much easier, both in the gaining of information and in the processing of it.

Types of surveys

Personal interviews

A personal interview is probably the most common type of survey used by trainers. The trainer has a prepared list of questions to discuss during the interview. This type of interview has the advantage of being reasonably flexible in its structure. The interviewer may decide to skip a question and come back to it later if it seems that there is more information to be gained this way from the person being interviewed.

Personal interviews are time-consuming, but they tend to be among the most accurate in their results. They are also a good 'networking' exercise for the new trainer.

Mail questionnaires

Mail questionnaires are an effective way of asking questions of a large group of people, or a number of groups that are geographically isolated. The design of the questions in this case needs to be very explicit and easy to understand. If the receivers do not correctly understand what it is you are asking, they will not answer appropriately.

Mail questionnaires are relatively simple to design and conduct. However, they are very impersonal and usually the response rates leave a lot to be desired.

Telephone interviews

A telephone interview is probably best described as a mix of the personal interview and the mail questionnaire. The telephone interview has a structured set of questions for the interviewer to ask, but it does not allow the flexibility of the personal interview. This is partly because the interviewer cannot observe or read the interviewee's body language and also because the interviewee is generally reluctant to ask for clarification of a question if that will extend the phone call.

The telephone interview is not commonly used in the gaining of information for a training needs analysis. It does have its place, but this place is limited in its uses.

Whom do we survey?

In nearly all surveys either all of the target population is surveyed or a selected number within the target group is sampled.

When we survey the total target population we get information from all the people with the specific characteristics that make them a distinct group. An example of this would be to survey all of the people employed as senior managers by the government.

When a few people within the larger group are selected for survey, we are sampling that group. When we are sampling, we must be aware of the factors that could give us misleading results in our survey. The sample must be a representative subset of the larger group. Following our example above, we would ensure that if we were going to sample these senior managers we would make certain to include the same percentage of females and country-based people in our sample as is indicated in our total population of senior managers. This is a simplistic example and there would be many other factors to consider when selecting the sample.

If we survey the total group or population we should get a very accurate answer. However, because this could prove to be an expensive project we have good reason to use a sample instead. If the sample has been calculated correctly we will still have accurate results and at a much reduced cost.

It is worth noting that usually when a survey is conducted the response is not as complete as anticipated. It becomes far too expensive to follow up the stragglers, so do not be tempted to achieve a 100 per cent response to your survey.

With mail questionnaires we need to consider a couple of items that may help to increase the response rate. The presentation of your questionnaire will have a significant bearing on the response rate. There should be a covering letter explaining the purpose of the survey and what is going to happen to the responses. It should also tell the respondent whether the responses will be confidential or not.

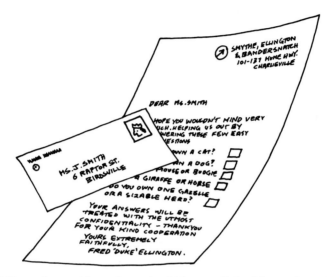

Addressed prepaid envelopes should be supplied with questionnaires

If the covering letter is to be signed, give it a personal touch by signing each one individually. It is also important to select a good quality paper for the material to be printed on. The layout of the questionnaire also needs to be tidy and easy to follow. Even if you supply addressed prepaid envelopes, which you should, don't be too surprised at the poor response in some cases.

Selecting questions

There are a number of issues that we have to consider when formulating the questions for a survey or interview. The questions have to be straightforward; they need to be designed to extract the maximum amount of information possible; they need to bemeaningful to the respondent; and they need to be put into language that everyone being asked can understand. Leading questions should be avoided. We don't want the respondents to be too limited in their responses and we don't want to ask questions that are irrelevant.

So we do have to consider quite a few items and this is only the beginning. You may decide to include many more when you start designing your own questions.

Before carrying out any survey, whether it be a personal interview, a mail questionnaire or a telephone interview, the questions must be tested. This exercise is called *piloting*. We pilot our questions to make sure that they are understood, and understood as we intended. If one person doesn't understand exactly what you want, others might not either. If there is any misinterpretation of the question, don't try to defend it, change it.

When the questions are piloted make sure that they are given to people from the correct population. Make sure, too, that you are administering the questions as you will in the real situation. When the questions have been completed, go back through them with your respondent question by question. Ask what was unclear or difficult and also ask if there should have been any other choices in pre-coded multiple-choice questions.

Conclusion

Of the three methods described in this chapter, two are used most commonly—the personal interview and the mail questionnaire. There are a number of other survey methods and techniques available, but they are not used as often as the three we have discussed here. If you intend to spend a great deal of time surveying it may also be of benefit to use group discussions, observation techniques and focus groups. However, for the normal survey being conducted for a training needs analysis by a relatively new trainer, the methods looked at here will be more than sufficient.

Application example

When we were asked to do a training needs analysis on a medium sized business we decided to use the questionnaire, followed up with personal interviews. This format was used as some of the offices involved were scattered around the country and it seemed to be the most cost effective solution. The questionnaire was intended to identify problems in the company, and the personal interviews, conducted with selected staff, were to determine if the problem was a training problem or a non-training problem.

A comprehensive questionnaire was formulated and is shown below. After being piloted with two of the staff members it was modified and then sent to all employees including those of management level.

When we started receiving the completed questionnaires, it was obvious to us that the questionnaire wasn't as comprehensive as we had originally thought. It was agreed that our follow-up personal interviews needed to be revised and had to cover the areas missed in the questionnaire.

When the personal interviews were completed all of the information from both the questionnaires and the personal interviews was collated, written out and given to the management with our recommendations.

It was interesting to note that the problems identified within the company were not all training problems and could not all be solved by training alone. However the final decision was in the hands of management.

All information given by the participants was treated in strict confidence. A copy of the questionnaire sent to all staff is shown below.

-1-

We have been asked to look into this company's (and your) training needs.

To assist us in making your work less stressful and more enjoyable, we are requesting that you answer the following questions.

There are two steps you'll need to make in order to complete each question. Firstly, you will need to determine your current level of skill for the task or skill indicated (this will be indicated by placing a 'P' in the spot selected). Secondly, you will need to determine your required level of the task or skill (this will be indicated by placing a 'T' in the spot selected).

We have an example below for you to look at:

John thinks that at present he has an average ability to manage his time (P = present). He also thinks that he should have a very high level of ability to manage his time (T = target).

	1	2	3	4	5	6

Managing time effectively .... ◯—◯—◯—Ⓟ—◯—Ⓣ

Note: 1 = Absent (No Knowledge)
2 = Very Low
3 = Quite Low
4 = Medium (Average)
5 = Quite High
6 = Very High (Expert)

. . . continued

-2-

	1	2	3	4	5	6
Managing time effectively	O—O—O—O—O—O
Understanding forms used	O—O—O—O—O—O
Understanding how to fill them in	O—O—O—O—O—O
Courier procedures	O—O—O—O—O—O
Maintenance procedures for vans	O—O—O—O—O—O
How we should schedule our time	O—O—O—O—O—O
Understanding of company	O—O—O—O—O—O
Handling difficult customers	O—O—O—O—O—O
Training other staff	O—O—O—O—O—O
Records and what to do with them	O—O—O—O—O—O
How company can expand with your help ...	O—O—O—O—O—O
Staff selection procedures	O—O—O—O—O—O
Needs analysis methods	O—O—O—O—O—O
Computer systems	O—O—O—O—O—O
Handling and loading of parcels	O—O—O—O—O—O
Driving skills	O—O—O—O—O—O

We would like to thank you for your time in answering these questions. The information that you have supplied to us will be treated in strict confidence and will only be used to establish training requirements.

A courier has been arranged to pick up the completed questionnaires next Monday. Would you please leave yours with the receptionist for collection before that date.

We will pass the end results of this questionnaire on to the staff when the information has been sorted.

Gary Kroehnert
Consultant.

Further reading

Baird, L., Schneier, C. & Laird, D., *The Training and Development Sourcebook*, Human Resource Press, Massachusetts, 1985, Part 1, Section II.

Cohen, L. & Manion, L., *Research Methods in Education*, Croom Helm, London, 1980.

Laird, Dugan, *Approaches to Training and Development*, Addison-Wesley Publishing Company, Massachusetts, 1978, Chapter 5.

Reeves, T. & Harper, D., *Surveys at Work*, McGraw-Hill Book Company, London, 1981.

Zemke, R. & Kramlinger, T., *Figuring Things Out: A Trainer's Guide to Needs and Task Analysis*, Addison-Wesley Publishing Company, Massachusetts, 1981.

CHAPTER 4

Location of training

The location, or training venue, is of major importance to both the trainer and the trainee. Unfortunately, the venue is not always given the attention it deserves; it tends to be taken for granted. For learning to take place effectively, we need to create a comfortable learning atmosphere.

Traditionally, we think about classrooms or training rooms when we talk about education or learning. But what about the possibility of conducting outdoor based learning activities? For learning to take place effectively we need to create not only a comfortable learning environment, but an appropriate one.

At the end of this section is a comprehensive checklist for indoor training venues. Chapter 26 has further information on outdoor based learning. It may include items that the experienced trainer may not be concerned with, but the new trainer will find it worthwhile checking all of the items listed.

Probably one of the most important features that trainers would like to see incorporated in training room design is the flexibility to arrange the room as a lecture theatre, or a discussion room, or as a number of workstation areas. Unfortunately we are not given this opportunity very often as we tend to exceed everyone's budget. If given the opportunity to choose or modify a training venue there are a number of things the trainer must take into consideration. Listed below are the items that we need to think of.

The number of participants generally determines the training location. A decision about the location should be the trainer's first priority. Don't try to squeeze a few more into an already crowded venue; cut the number down or get another location. A crowded venue will not set the proper learning atmosphere. Similarly, a large room for just a few people can also create a barrier to learning.

The size of the training room will generally depend on two factors: what the room is being used for and the number of people it has to accommodate. If the room is being used in a classroom setting (a chair with arm tables), allow about 2 to 2.5 square metres per person. If the room is being used in a conference setting (chairs and full tables) allow about 2.5 to 3.5 square metres per person. A simple method of estimating the size of the room needed is to multiply the number of participants by the area required per person, then add a bit for yourself and your equipment. It is possible to find many other specifications for training room sizes, but they vary greatly. An alternative is to use a room that is a size you and the group feel comfortable with. For your first few sessions check with an experienced trainer in your organization for advice on room sizes and limits to participants in your training rooms. The information given to you will probably be close to the first alternative described.

The arrangement of the room needs to suit the training program. Try to keep things looking tidy. If you're conducting a lecture, keep the front of the room clear for the lecturer. If there will be a lot of small-group work, arrange the seating roughly where you want the groups to be located. Ensure that the arrangements allow for everyone to see and hear adequately.

Suitable chairs and tables are needed for a classroom situation. The chairs must be comfortable but firm. (If they're too comfortable, you may lose a few participants as they nod off.) The tables should be narrow and long, about 0.5 by 1.8 metres, which allows the participants to sit two wide along the table on one side. Don't be tempted to increase the number of participants by sitting them on both sides of the table, as it gets too crowded.

The arrangement of chairs and tables generally sets the scene for the participants. If they see the chairs set in a circle they should expect a lot of group discussion. If they see the chairs set in rows they could expect that the trainer will be doing most of the work.

The lighting in the room must be arranged to provide for both the trainer's and trainees' requirements. The trainer needs light for the whiteboard to be seen (but not so much that it becomes hard or for the trainees to see the overhead projector screen). The trainees also need enough light to be able to take notes if they require. It up to the individual trainer to determine the lighting requirements.

Noise in the background during training can be very destructive to the learning atmosphere. Most trainers would like to have a totally soundproof room without any windows, but unfortunately this type of room is rare.

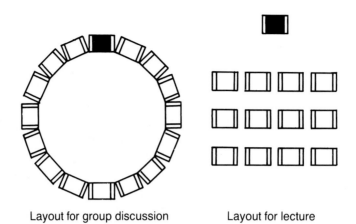

Layout for group discussion   Layout for lecture

Seating arrangements should be suitable for the intended training method

What we can do, though, is locate the training room far enough away from the work area to exclude work noises such as machines and telephones.

The temperature of the training room must be comfortable for the majority of the group. Don't try to satisfy everyone, you won't be able to. Keep the temperature between 20°C and 25°C if possible, and also allow for gentle air circulation in the room. It is strongly recommended that smoking be banned in any classroom situation. Not only might the smoke be hard on your voice but some of the other participants might feel very uncomfortable with it. Another thing to remember is that some training aids generate heat during their use, and your cooling equipment must be able to handle this problem.

Access is something that most trainers now take for granted, but we do need to consider how the participants will get to the venue. Will public transport be sufficient? If they use their own transport will they have somewhere to park? We must also consider access for the disabled, such as ramps for wheelchairs.

The facilities that we usually now take for granted must be checked by the trainer. Are tea and coffee making facilities available for morning and afternoon breaks? Do we have access to telephones? Do we know where all the toilets are located? Do we know where the fire exits are? All of this information must be passed on to the participants at the beginning of the course. It may also be necessary to find out if there is residential accommodation available.

Distractions, apart from noise and temperature, might also be present. Participants can find irrelevant posters and paintings on the walls a distraction. A room painted an unusual colour can be a distraction. Windows can be a source of participant distraction, so check to see if blinds can be used to reduce this problem. A crowded room can be a distraction and the trainer must fix this before training starts. Anything that is not required for the session to be conducted should be removed from the training room so as not to attract attention.

The acoustic qualities of the location should assist the leader in keeping control of the group. The trainer's voice should be the dominant noise in the room. If the acoustics are good, background noise should be minimal. The noise from background conversation and projectors should be absorbed by the room, and not be in competition with the speaker.

Power outlets must be checked for availability and location. If you are going to train in a new location check the power outlets. Their location may affect your arrangement of the room.

Training aids must be checked to see that the ones you want to use are available. Some training and conference facilities have only a limited type and quantity. When you establish that the training aids you require are available, check to make sure they are in top working condition. And do it yourself, don't take anyone's word for it.

Spares must be located and you will need to know how to fit them. Overhead projectors, film projectors and slide projectors, for example, might have a globe burn out while you are using them. Prompt replacement means the least disruption.

A public-address system may be advisable in a large conference or seminar situation. It could be a portable type or a built-in system. If you believe that all of the people in the group will not be able to hear the speakers properly you must make enquiries into the use of the public address system.

Storage areas could be needed for excess equipment, student handouts, training aids not in use, spare parts, training models and many other items.

```
┌─────────────────────────────────────────────────────────┐
│ VENUE CHECKLIST                                         │
├─────────────────────────────────────────────────────────┤
│ Number of participants                        ————      │
│ Size of room                                  ————      │
│ Arrangement of room                           ————      │
│ Suitable chairs and tables                    ————      │
│ Arrangement of furniture                      ————      │
│ Lighting                                      ————      │
│ Noise                                         ————      │
│ Temperature                                   ————      │
│ Access                                        ————      │
│ Facilities                                    ————      │
│ Distractions on walls                         ————      │
│ Distractions outside                          ————      │
│ Acoustic qualities                            ————      │
│ Power outlets                                 ————      │
│ Extension leads                               ————      │
│ Overhead projector                            ————      │
│ Whiteboard and markers                        ————      │
│ Video and monitor                             ————      │
│ Projection equipment                          ————      │
│ Spares                                        ————      │
│ PA system                                     ————      │
│ Storage area                                  ————      │
│                                                         │
│ _____             ————      │
│ _____             ————      │
│ _____             ————      │
│ _____             ————      │
│ _____             ————      │
└─────────────────────────────────────────────────────────┘
```

Conclusion

The training venue needs to have a learning atmosphere created by the trainer. If we don't create this atmosphere, there may be a barrier which prevents learning from taking place.

The training location doesn't have to have state-of-the-art equipment, but it does need to be a suitable size for the group and to be set out to suit the use intended. The design should be flexible to some extent, allow for adequate ventilation, have satisfactory lighting and have suitable facilities. This is the minimum standard that trainers should allow for the participants as well as for themselves.

With some venues, trainers need to use their imagination and creativity to overcome some enormous problems so that they can create a suitable learning climate. Without this atmosphere we may as well pack up and go home.

Application example

Next month you may be required to conduct a training programme for your organization in an unfamiliar city. To find a suitable venue you will first need to determine the number of participants who will be attending. This will allow you to work out roughly what size room is needed.

With this information it is now possible to contact a number of locations and request full information about their facilities. When you receive the information you will be able to go through your checklist and check off most of the items. This will generally be enough information to make a decision on which venue to use.

It is your responsibility to check the outstanding items at the location before any training commences.

Further reading

Baird, L., Schneier, C. & Laird, D., *The Training and Development Sourcebook*, Human Resource Press, Massachusetts, 1985, Section VII, B.

Craig, Robert, *Training and Development Handbook*, 2nd edn, McGraw-Hill Book Company, New York, 1976, Chapter 7.

Laird, Dugan, *Approaches to Training and Development*, Addison-Wesley Publishing Company, Massachusetts, 1978, Chapter 12.

CHAPTER 5

Researching a topic

In this chapter we will be looking at the research that may be required in preparation for the presentation of a new session. This is different from the research for a needs analysis which was covered in Chapter 2.

Research into a topic is generally conducted for at least two reasons: firstly, to supply information for the session to be presented and, secondly, to give the researcher some expert information on the topic.

Why is research necessary?

The participants must be given correct and up-to-date information in each presentation they attend. The best way for the trainer to find out if it is correct and up-to-date is to spend some time researching the relevant facts.

Careful research makes for a well prepared trainer

Also, the participants rightly expect the trainer to know thoroughly the topics being presented. Would you sit and listen attentively to a trainer who did not appear to know the subject? This means that the trainer must carry out study before entering the training room. Experienced trainers will tell you that unless the subject matter is completely understood by them they cannot effectively plan their presentation or communicate confidently to the participants.

Trainers must learn how to confine their research to a useable quantity

Don't think that you have to be a walking encyclopaedia, or an authority on every subject you will be presenting. But you must know more about the subject than you will be presenting to the participants. You will find that this information may be needed to answer some of the questions that will be asked. Considering the rate at which information is currently being generated on most topics, we probably all find that we simply haven't got the time to keep totally up to date.

If you find that you are asked a question relevant to the topic and you don't know the answer to it, tell the group that you don't know but that you will find out and report back to them later.

What methods are available?

I know I said before that this chapter was to discuss researching a topic rather than research for a needs analysis, but we will find that, depending on the subject matter, many sources may be common to both.

Sources of research for a presentation may include:

- activity figures, such as production, sales, wastage, quality control
- staff performance appraisal records
- job analysis, including job descriptions and work study reports

- relevant policies and procedures
- interview records with the employees, their supervisors and any other personnel involved
- personnel evaluations, such as employee test results, questionnaires, lists of identified competencies
- the workplace itself, such as equipment, supplies, technology, work processes, raw material, etc.
- corporate plans, such as those for new technology, expansion or contraction, diversification, mergers
- accident reports and statistics.

While these sources provide ample information for a training needs analysis, they may provide only a small amount of information on a particular topic or subject. Perhaps this information is ample for your needs, but if you find that you require more information on your subject, the following research sources may be useful.

A library can provide bulk information, but trying to wade through it all can be a problem in itself. Don't try to read and understand it all; ask the librarian for assistance in narrowing your broad topic down to a manageable size. Computers may also be used effectively for this purpose. Not all libraries carry the same books; most now specialize in different subjects. Make sure you find out which one you need to visit.

A film library may give you a change of pace for your research and presentation. If you find a relevant film or video on your topic you may decide to use it in your presentation after you have previewed it. The number of film libraries is continually increasing and they are relatively easy to locate.

Advertisements in the magazines and publications you subscribe to may give you other starting points for sources of information.

The personnel section may be able to tell you of employees who are knowledgable in the subject you are researching. If the information required is job related, they may even be able to give you the names of retired personnel who worked in certain areas for a number of years. These people can be a tremendous source of information.

Specialists who are known to have information in your subject may be contacted. Consultants and professional educators are examples of such specialists but the main problem is trying to get them to give you some of their time. You may find that some specialists have their own libraries of books and films. As these have already been selectively chosen they could also be of use, particularly if you can get recommendations from the specialist as to which ones you need to look at.

Old records located in your organization can unveil relevant reference documents, and if you're lucky perhaps some slides or photographs you may be able to use in your presentation.

Relevant trades areas normally have condensed information in booklet form that maybe used for your research. You may also find that they have produced films or videos that could be of value to you and your participants.

Government agencies that deal with training, education and employment are also useful sources of information. It may take some time to find what you're looking for, but it will generally be worth the effort.

Staff are often overlooked as sources of information for your research. Have you ever asked the people around you what qualifications and experience they have? Ask them sometime, you may get a pleasant surprise.

If you have used more than a couple of these sources for your research, you may find that you now have so much information you don't know how you're going to present it all. The solution is easy—you don't present it all. What you need to do now is to sort all of your expert research information into different categories. You want to select the information the trainees *must* know to be able to carry out what will be required of them.

You may find that before you start your research, it is worthwhile designing some type of filing system. As you find sources of information for particular topics (not necessarily the one you are currently researching), record them on a topic card or something similar. You may find at a later date that you need to research a topic that is already in your files. If so, some of the hard work is already done for you.

Conclusion

It is important for you as the trainer to know as much about the subject matter as would be expected by the participants. If you want to have any credibility with them, and if you want them to become involved and motivated, you need to become more than just conversant with the subject material.

The research exercise can become very tiring in some cases. However, if you're asked, or told, to present a session where you don't know the topic material very well, it's definitely in your best interests to research the material thoroughly.

You may find that when you start your research, the job is easiest if you break your large topic area into smaller specific sub-topics. This will save a lot of time as you will only be dealing with relevant information.

When you finish your research, remember to cull the information you have collected so that you finish up with only the material that the participants must know in connection with the topic. If you have more session time than is required, you may start giving them some of the secondary information, but remember that it's better to teach a small amount well than to teach a large amount not so well.

Application example

Let's say that you have been given the job of researching a presentation on 'Safe lifting practices in the workplace'. Assuming that you had very little knowledge of the topic, what sources would you use to carry out your research?

If you go back over the sources listed in this chapter, you should be able to identify at least fifteen separate sources. In addition to those listed you could probably think of at least half a dozen more. See how easy it is to become overloaded with research information?

Now comes the step of refining the information down to that which is essential to the participants. With the information sorted, you may now prepare your presentation being confident that you have a more than satisfactory knowledge of the material.

Further reading

Craig, Robert, *Training and Development Handbook*, 2nd edn, McGraw-Hill Book Company, New York, 1976, Chapter 44.

CHAPTER 6

Objectives

This chapter is probably one of the most important in this book, particularly for the new trainer. The reason for making such a strong statement is that without clearly stated objectives the trainer and the trainee may have absolutely no idea of where they are heading. If they don't know where they are heading, how can they know when they have reached their target? Very simply, an objective, or a number of objectives, give us our target, or learning goals. This target or goal will apply to the individual session or to the course of instruction as a whole. All of the session objectives taken together should equal the course objective/s.

Ch.2→ All training objectives are normally designed and written after the training needs analysis has been completed, a training need has been identified, and the decision to go ahead with the program has been made.

We will be talking in later chapters about using 'road maps' for the design and delivery of sessions. If we apply the idea of a 'road map' to this chapter our objective is the finishing point.

Make sure that you map out the course you intend a session to take

The difference between aims and objectives

Even experienced trainers can sometimes become confused between aims and objectives. Aims and objectives are not the same thing. An aim normally consists of a statement of general intent. It may use an item or example to represent the final approvable behaviour of the participant at the conclusion

Keep the aims and objectives of the session clearly in mind

of the course or workshop. By contrast, an objective states the requirements in precise terms. An example of this might be:

Session Aim: To develop an awareness and understanding of the different types of training methods.

Session Objective: By the end of this session participants will be able to correctly list at least twenty different training methods (stating one advantage and disadvantage for each) using the notes provided.

The above example shows that the aim simply states a general intent which would probably be useful in promoting or selling the course or workshop to the management or the participants. The session objective would normally be given to the participants at the beginning of the session so that they know exactly what is required of them by the end of the session.

To use the road map analogy again: the aim tells us what town we are going to; the objective tells us which street, what time we need to be there and what the road conditions are.

When do we need objectives?

After it has been established that someone needs training, we know in a general way, what subjects or topics need to be included in the training program from the results of the training needs analysis. When we know what subject matter is to be covered, we need to sit down and write general instructional objectives for the course, followed by specific session objectives for each separate session.

We can't start to write any of the teaching material for the course until we have established the session objectives, otherwise we risk the chance of the information being on the wrong track. How do we know which road to take if we don't know where we're going? As well as being important for the trainer, when specific objectives are stated to the group members, they can also be certain in which direction we should all be headed. How many times have you been sitting in a presentation and had absolutely no idea where the presenter was heading, or when, or if, they had reached the objective of the session?

If we are using other presenters, they must be given specific session objectives so they will know what the outcome must be. Without these objectives they won't know what exactly needs to be covered.

An example of this may be the situation where we ask a fellow trainer to present a session on 'video recorders', and they deliver a session on 'how a video recorder operates'. What was really wanted should have been described in a clearly stated objective: 'At the end of this session the participants must be able to label the components in a given diagram of a video recorder with 100 per cent accuracy'. See how much easier the task has been made for everyone?

Another important reason for using course and session objectives is that they give us a base for any form of evaluation or test we intend to apply. If we state our objective clearly it tells us what the evaluation must be. If the test or evaluation doesn't tie in exactly with the objectives, one of them must be modified so that they do match each other.

How do we write an objective?

Probably the hardest thing about training is to formulate the session or the course objectives. We must assume that if we put all of the session objectives together they will equal the course objective.

All objectives should be stated in observable behavior or performance and should not merely describe what the participants have learnt or become familiar with during the time allocated for the course. There is a second requirement for an objective; it should be measurable in some form so that we can set our tests from it. It can therefore be said that objectives should be both observable and measurable.

It is generally believed that reaching our session objectives will eventually lead to us achieving the desired behavioral change or attitude change.

Writing objectives can be confusing at first for the new trainer and not all experienced trainers find writing objectives a simple task. It may be simplest to start writing your objectives by filling in the missing spaces in the formula below:

By the end of this session the trainee will be able to

_____ (an action word) _____

_____ (item) _____

_____ (condition) _____

_____ (standard) _____

The *action word* is something we can observe; the *item* is normally an object or item from our session; the *condition* is what's given and describes any variables; and the *standard* is our measurable criteria. (To help you there is a list of terms you can select from at the end of this chapter.) To give you an example:

> By the end of this session the trainee will be able to
> underline (an action word)
> the nouns (item)
> given a printed list of statements (condition)
> and have at least 80 per cent correct. (standard)

Another one:

> By the end of this session the trainee will be able to
> total (an action word)
> a list of numbers (item)
> given a prepared sheet and a calculator (condition)
> and have at least 90 per cent correct. (standard)

One more:

> By the end of this session the trainee will be able to
> assemble (an action word)
> the parts of an overhead projector (item)
> given all of the parts in a box and without the aid of a manufacturer's manuals. (condition)
> The project must be in assembled working order within ten minutes. (standard)

Just to make sure:

> By the end of this session the trainee will be able to
> demonstrate (an action word)
> the procedure for assembling a DT5 (item)
> given all of the unassembled parts and the manufacturer's technical manuals. (condition)

to the manufacturer's specification within three hours. (standard)
And finally:
  By the end of this session the trainee will be able to
  count (an action word)
  the number of needles in a haystack (item)
  given a haystack, a magnet, a magnifying glass and a box of band aids
    (condition)
  The counting must be completed within twelve hours, and must be
    correct. (standard)

Conclusion

Why should we use objectives in training?

- They provide direction.
- They provide guidelines for testing.
- They convey instructional intent to others.

When we sit down to write our objectives we must ensure that we set realistic goals. The objectives must be achievable within the constraints placed on us, whether these relate to time, resources, facilities or any other factor likely to affect the final outcome.

After the results of the training needs analysis have been interpreted, we can state that certain objectives have to be reached within the program. Nearly all objectives are set after we have conducted the training needs analysis.

We also use our stated objectives to set the test criteria, which must match them. It's not uncommon for the test to be written straight after the objectives have been designed. With these starting and finishing points established, it becomes relatively easy to fill in the gap. With this method we can be certain that the test is in line with the objective.

A well-written and easily understood objective must:

- state something about the end of the session or the end of training
- say something about the trainee, not the instructor or the course
- include an input or a condition
- have single outcomes
- state a performance by using action words
- include a standard to be achieved by the trainee
- be stated in such a way that there is no doubt as to what is required.

At the conclusion of a course or session that may be conducted again, it is good practice for the trainer to consider revising the objective. It may be that the objective, as stated, is unachievable or is not challenging enough. Review it while the experience of the training is still fresh in your mind.

The final list of objectives should contain outcomes that are considered essential for the trainees to achieve. These objectives are usually the minimum standards that the trainee should reach. It may be that they are the minimum requirements needed for the trainee to move on to the next area of learning.

I deliberately have not used any quotations so far in this book. Sometimes they seem inappropriate and serve merely to fill up space. However I have a quote for you now as I believe that this is a very relevant statement made by an expert on objectives, Robert Mager, in his book *Preparing Instructional Objectives*.

"The purpose of the objective is to communicate something to somebody. If that somebody doesn't get the message as intended, don't argue or defend—fix it!"

Don't get hung up on the terms unless it's required specifically for some reason. The main thing is to make sure it's all covered!

Application example

Some months ago a trainer I know was asked to develop a trainer training course. After a training needs analysis had been carried out, it appeared that there were several topic areas requiring certain amounts of information. When all of this information had been gathered and sorted, session objectives had to be written and were given to the presenting trainers. The trainers, having been given these specific session objectives, then knew the goal/s they, and the trainees, had to reach by the end of the sessions. The following are a few of the session objectives that were written and handed over to the trainers.

- By the end of this session the participants will be able to state (without referring to notes) at least fifteen items that need to be taken into consideration for a training venue.
- By the end of this session the participants will be able to correctly (without reference) demonstrate the assembly and operation of a video camera and recorder in the training room.
- By the end of this session the participants will be able to write a set of session notes for a given topic using the sample format that will be handed out. The finished notes must be understood by the instructor without explanation.

Are these objectives stated correctly?

List of common action words

add	arrange	assemble	bend
build	calculate	carry	catch
choose	circle	collect	colour
compute	construct	count	cut
demonstrate	describe	design	divide
draw	fold	identify	illustrate
indicate	label	lift	list
mark	match	modify	multiply
name	perform	pick	place
plan	point	punctuate	rearrange
recall	recite	rewrite	ride
run	select	separate	smile
solve	spell	state	swim
tabulate	taste	throw	translate
underline	use	walk	write

List of common terms for standards

Accurate to _____ decimal points
At least 8 out of 10 attempts
At least _____ per cent correct
At least _____ within an hour
At _____ per hour
Before sunset
Having all correct
In the specified sequence
Not acceptable if safety procedures are violated
With at least _____ correct
Within _____ minutes
Within _____ tolerance
Without error
With no more than _____ errors

List of common terms for equipment to use (conditions)

Given a checklist, notes and manual
Given a complete technical manual
Given a set of blueprints
Given a slide rule
Standing on your head
Under simulated conditions
Using all of the parts
Using any equipment needed
Using the machine practised on
Using your notes
Without the use of a manual
Without the use of a calculator
With the aid of a checklist

Further reading

Baird, L., Schneier, C. & Laird, D., *The Training and Development Source-book*, Human Resource Press, Massachusetts, 1985, Part 1, Section V.

Donaldson, Les & Scannell, Edward, *Human Resource Development: The New Trainer's Guide*, 2nd edn, Addison-Wesley Publishing Company, Massachusetts, 1986, Chapter 4.

Gronlund, Norman, *Stating Objectives for Classroom Instruction*, 3rd edn, Macmillan Publishing, New York, 1985.

Laird, Dugan, *Approaches to Training and Development*, Addison-Wesley Publishing Company, Massachusetts, 1978, Chapter 8.

Mager, Robert, *Preparing Instructional Objectives*, 2nd edn, Pitman Learning Company, California, 1984.

CHAPTER 7

Demonstrating a skill

The formal lecture has little use in skill or practical training, where muscular and manual activities demand that learning is done by doing.

In a skill training session the demonstrator must aim to have the participants perform the skill correctly the first time. Another aim should be to get the students to develop smooth, confident and easy movements when performing the skill. During the skill session the instructor must also promote accuracy, speed and quality.

This chapter will look at two topics dealing with the demonstration of a skill:

- What is a skill?
- How do you go about demonstrating a skill correctly?

At the end of this chapter is a copy of a skill session sheet which may be of use to the skills trainer.

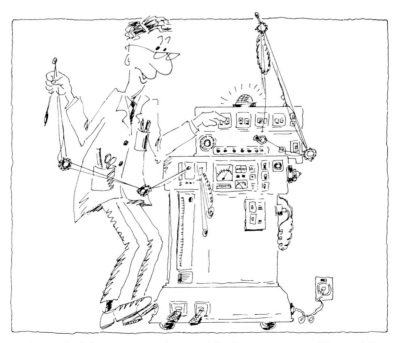

A practical demonstration is essential when you are teaching a skill

43

What is a skill?

A skill is a complex sequence of practical activities. Some examples of skills would include typing, washing up, cleaning a white board, plugging in an overhead projector or turning on a light.

Some skills are far more complex than others. Some may only involve some simple motion such as turning on an overhead projector. Others may involve the use of the senses, such as determining whether an overhead image is being projected squarely onto the screen or not. The more complex type of skill could involve understanding and knowledge, for example, the ability to read the operating instructions of the overhead projector and to understand them.

It can be seen that almost everything that is done using some form of motion is a skill. As most activities use all three types of skills (motor, perceptual and cognitive) we will deal with them as a combined activity. This combination of motor, perceptual and cognitive skills is given the term 'psychomotor skill'. Regardless of the type of skill that you may be demonstrating, the rules remain the same.

Skills training always involves the same basic rules

Demonstrating a skill correctly

The complete demonstration process involves four sections, these are:

- preparation
- demonstration
- student practice
- assessment.

We will look at all of these sections in one process as they must go hand-in-hand.

The steps:

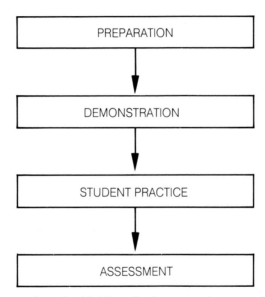

The trainer's procedure should follow the demonstration—practice sequence for any skills training

The preparation

There is a great deal the demonstrator must do before demonstrating a skill to any group. Some of the items that need to be attended to will include the following:

- establishing the current level of knowledge of the trainees in the given topic/subject as they may not have the prerequisite knowledge to perform the skill
- discussing the skill with other 'experts', analysing the skill and breaking it down

- drafting a plan to be followed for the demonstration so all relevant points can be covered in logical sequence
- preparing all training support materials such as overhead transparencies, handouts, samples, films, videos, models, project lists, examinations, marking guides
- preparing lesson objectives and building in links back and forward to other areas of instruction or other fields
- preparation of an introduction. A good introduction will gain attention, arouse interest in the demonstration, and check existing knowledge.

The trainer's personal preparation is a major part of skill training

This is not intended to be a comprehensive list of items to be carried out by the demonstrator, but it does show that the demonstrator has to be prepared in many ways to demonstrate a skill correctly and professionally.

Practical instruction is like an iceberg, in that the part that is visible (conducting a demonstration and supervising student practice) makes up only a small part of the effort. The bulk of the work goes on beforehand.

The demonstration

The demonstration *must* be done correctly. How can anyone expect a trainee to do it correctly if the demonstrator can't?

There are a few methods suggested for the sequence of demonstrations. We will be discussing the one that tends to be the most commonly referred to in current texts, and is being used by many adult colleges.

The method has seven basic steps. They are easy to follow and they also cover the final two sections of our process, student practice and assessment.

1 **Demonstrate at normal speed.**
Demonstrate the skill correctly, at normal speed, so that the trainee can see the final result and can also see what is expected from them at the conclusion of training.

2 **Demonstrate again slowly.**
Demonstrate again for the trainees, this time doing it slowly so that they can see exactly what is being done. As the trainer demonstrates, the student should begin to recognize names, parts, tools and any obvious skills.

When demonstrating and explaining how the skill is performed, trainers must be careful about what they say and how they say it. The trainer should introduce each step, then highlight the key points with deliberate and possibly exaggerated movements. These key points can also be highlighted by voice, by giving reasons, or perhaps by repetition. It's a good idea to pause between key points to let them sink in. The demonstrator must have a set of notes or a 'skill sheet' to follow for this part of the demonstration. The skill sheet gives a complete breakdown of the skill, with the key points highlighted and any 'tricks of the trade' and safety points noted.

3 **Verbal instruction from the trainees.**
Now get the trainees to tell you how to carry out the task in the correct sequence. The demonstrator carries out the performance as instructed by the trainees.

Student practice

4 **Controlled trainee performance.**
Have the trainees carry out the skill under close supervision and at a controlled pace. It is important that the trainees perform this exercise correctly. It is difficult, and sometimes almost impossible, to counteract the effects of a skill learned incorrectly.

5 **Student practice.**
Now is the time for student practice. This part of a skill session should be at least 50 per cent of the allocated session time. During

this time the demonstrator must be available to answer any questions that arise. If a trainee has problems don't take over from them but get them to fix it themselves; the trainer or other members of the group can give the correct information or suggestions. Try also to enlist their peers to assist with any problems.

The assessment

6 **Student assessment.**

Some form of assessment must take place to ensure that the trainees have reached the stated objectives and standards that were described at the beginning of the session.

Assessment may be done during the session by asking questions, or it may be done at the end of the session by using some form of test (written, practical or other). The type of assessment generally depends on the demonstrator and the type of skill being instructed. The test could be getting the trainee to replace the globe in an overhead projector to the manufacturer's standards within fifteen seconds.

An important point with assessment is that trainees should be expecting the type of test you give. The test must also be relevant to the topic. If you are demonstrating how to change a globe in an overhead projector, get them to change the globe. Don't give them a test that asks them to identify all of the parts of the projector.

7 **Conclusion.**

The session must conclude with the demonstrator recapitulating the main points of the session, and clarifying any outstanding areas of concern. If possible, all test results should be made available before the end of the session, so they might be included in the conclusion.

To demonstrate a skill correctly:

---

1 Demonstrate at normal speed
2 Demonstratte again slowly
3 Verbal instruction from the trainees
4 Controlled trainee performance
5 Student practice
6 Student assessment
7 Conclusion

Conclusion

The skill sheet has proven itself to be invaluable in the process of skill training. It ensures that the trainer covers all the relevant points in the correct sequence and it gives the key points and safety points at the right time. Trainers need to start out with clear objectives and must always be thinking of ways to motivate the participants to learn.

Trainers should design a skill sheet to suit their own needs. This is not uncommon and so there is a wide variety of types. Most of them are different and include only the information particular trainers require for their personal use. Samples are given at the end of this chapter.

Another important point to remember is that at least half the time in a demonstration session should be made available for trainees to perform and practise the skill. Also, remember that the first time trainees perform the skill it must be done correctly.

It is strongly suggested that the demonstrator practise the demonstration before giving the performance. It doesn't matter how well you think you know how to do it, sometimes the parts don't fit the way they should—so practise.

Application example

To trial this concept we gave a new instructor the task of demonstrating 'how to assemble and disassemble a SCUBA (Self Contained Underwater Breathing Apparatus) unit'. These particular skill sheets needed to be slightly different from most others as they were to be used by a number of scuba diving instructors and therefore had to be understood by all.

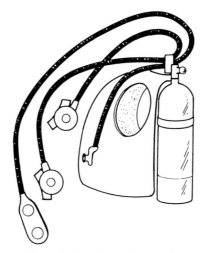

Skill training is applicable in a wide variety of situations

The first step for the instructor was to research the current information available on the particular subject, the main references being two instructor-level texts. These texts supplied only very basic information, which surprised the trainers who had assumed that the information would be more comprehensive. On completion of that assignment the instructor spoke to two other experienced scuba-diving instructors to obtain any relevant information they might have. This information was to highlight the safety points and tricks of the trade.

When the research and discussions had been finalised, it was time to practise performing the skill. While doing so the instructor made notes of the correct sequence to be followed by the students. These notes included a clearly stated objective, an introduction and a motivator for the group. As this set of notes was completed, a draft skill sheet was written to include the operations, key points and safety points. On completion of the main skill sheet, the front cover sheet was finalised and it included all the other necessary information, such as objectives, equipment needed, references and problems.

The final skill sheet was included with the session notes, the presentation went ahead and the notes used by the new instructor worked well. To check that the notes were easily understood by other instructors, it was decided to run the presentation a second time, with another instructor using the skill sheets. This again proved to be satisfactory, both for the instructor and the trainee.

Further reading

Field, Laurie, *Skilling Australia*, Longman Cheshire, Melbourne, 1990.

Field, Laurie, *Teaching Practical Work at TAFE*, Published by ITATE, Sydney, 1984.

Pennington, F. C., *Assessing Educational Needs of Adults*, New Directions for Continuing Education Quarterly Sourcebooks, Jossey-Bass, San Francisco, 1980, Series No. 7.

Video: *You'll Soon Get the Hang of It*, Video Arts.

Video: *Right First Time*, New South Wales TAFE.

SHEET NO. ....

TITLE/SKILL: ..Assembly and disassembly of SCUBA equipment ....

....

OBJECTIVE/S: ..By the end of this session students will be able to: ....
..1) attach a BCD to the scuba tank so that the pack is snug, ...
.....oriented in the proper direction, and placed at the correct ....
.....height ....
..2) attach a scuba regulator to a scuba tank so that the regulator ....
.....hose is oriented to come over the right shoulder and the low ....
.....pressure inflator is on the left ....
..3) attach the low pressure inflator hose correctly onto the BCD ....
.....and check the operation ....
..4) demonstrate correct procedure for checking tank pressure ....
.....and regulator operation ....
..5) explain suggested actions for a high pressure O-ring leak ....
.....and for a free-flowing regulator ....
..6) correctly remove a regulator from a scuba tank and replace ....
.....the dust cap on the regulator ....
..7) correctly remove the BCD from the scuba tank and place ....
.....both items on ground ....

EQUIPMENT: ..• 1 tank, regulator and BCD for each student and instructor ....
..• spare O-rings ....

....

REFERENCE: ..NAUI Professional Resource Organiser (1984) ....
.. Openwater 1 scuba diver Instructor Guide ....

PROBLEMS: .. • ensure regulators have low pressure inflator hoses ....
.. • ensure all tanks are fully charged ....

....

INTRODUCTION: ..If you want to be able to breath underwater you must be able to ....
..assemble your equipment correctly. This equipment involves the ....
..use of high pressure air and if not used correctly can cause ....
..serious injury ....

OPERATIONS:	KEY POINTS:	SAFETY:
ASSEMBLE Position tank	— Stand tank up — O-ring facing away	— Don't leave tank standing unattended
Position BCD	— Slide over tank — BCD facing away — Height of BCD should be ½ way up tank valve — Adjust to fit different size tanks (63 & 88) — Lock in position	— Avoid hitting head on tank valve — Must be secure so it doesn't fall out when straps are set
Position & attach regulator	— Remove dust cap — Regulator and octopus to right side — Machined face to O-ring — Do up finger tight — Connect low pressure inflator to BCD	— Keep out of sand — Check O-ring is there — If too tight cannot undo later — Pull knurled nut back
Turn air on	— Turn tank on — Check tank pressure — Check 2nd stage regulator — Check octopus — Check L.P. inflator	— Slowly check position of gauges On and back ½ turn What to do if O-ring mising — Must be full to commence dive — Must breath easily — Must inflate and deflate
Lay down	— Gauges and regulators in front	— Keep out of sand and grass
DISMANTLE		
To turn off	— Turn air off — Purge lines	— Not over tight
Remove regulator	— Disconnect L.P. inflator — Undo nut — Replace dust cap — Place regulator away	— Must be dry
	Remove BCD — Undo velcro — Slide off tank — Place BCD away	— Hold tank
Tank	— Lay tank down	— So it won't fall
FINAL		
Rinse all equipment		— Don't push purge button

Sheet no: _____

Title/Skill: _____
_____
_____

Objective/s: _____
_____
_____
_____
_____
_____
_____

Equipment: _____
_____
_____
_____
_____
_____

Reference: _____
_____
_____

Problems: _____
_____
_____

Introduction: _____
_____
_____
_____
_____
_____

Operations	Key points	Safety

CHAPTER 8

Session plans

In this chapter we will describe what session plans or lesson plans are, look at the reasons for having them and describe what they should include. At the end of this chapter you will find one form of session plan. It may be used until you choose to devise your own.

What are session plans?

Session plans are useful tools for trainers in any field. They ensure that the instructor heads towards the objective/s of the lesson. They also enable the trainer to check in advance that the sequencing of the lesson is correct, the content relevant, and the training methods suitable. The session plan is also a checklist of the resources required for the lesson.

A session plan is a set of notes in logical order for the instructor to follow to ensure that the objectives set for the lesson are met. A session plan also includes other relevant information such as the training aids required, references used and identified problem areas. A separate session plan must be used for each session because they all have their own objectives and each therefore requires separate planning. Generally it is a requirement that the lesson objectives be reached by the participants before moving on to the next lesson.

Why use session plans?

Why use a road map when going on a driving holiday? A session plan is very similar to a road map in that it shows us a starting point, a finishing point, and all the places we need to pass or explore along the way. Without the road map we would be able to start our journey, but we would not know where we were going, or if and when we had reached our destination.

As well as giving the instructor a logical list of information to be covered in a session and its appropriate sequence, a session plan also indicates the timing for the lesson. A well-designed session plan allows the trainer to revise the material prior to the lesson without spending time researching the topic again, and also allows another trainer to conduct the same lesson effectively.

A well-designed set of notes may also be used for legal purposes should the situation ever arise.

55

What should a session plan include?

Session plans normally include the following:

- a session title
- session objectives clearly stated
- total session times
- participant details
- potential faults to be aware of
- review notes of the previous session/s
- a need for the student to know
- method of presentation
- content of the lesson
- lists of new terms
- key questions to be asked
- resources required for the lesson
- timing for the lesson
- student activities
- a link forward to the next session.

When considering the subject matter, it is important to identify those things that the students 'must know', 'should know' and 'could know'. The 'must know' items are those that the student must know in order to perform the task or duty required. The 'should know' items are the things that *may* be needed if the student is to gain a clear understanding of the essential information. The 'could know' items are the things that may be desirable for clear understanding, but are not essential.

Look at the target on the following page. Using this target, our instruction is aimed at the 'must know' area. It would be reasonable to assume that if we aimed at the bull's eye a certain amount of time would also be spent in the 'should know' area. If time permits let the students look in the 'could know' area, but the time would probably be better spent reviewing the 'must knows' and 'should knows'. It is usually better to teach too little well, than to teach too much badly. It is up to the individual trainer to categorize information into these groups, but the task if made easier if you look at the course curriculum.

A lesson plan allows you to check in advance that the sequencing is correct, that the content is relevant, and that the intended methods of training are suitable. The lesson plan also acts as a resource checklist for the instructor. It also allows the instructor to prepare well in advance for any material that may be required for the lesson, such as handouts, films, overhead transparencies, videos, slides, projection equipment and samples.

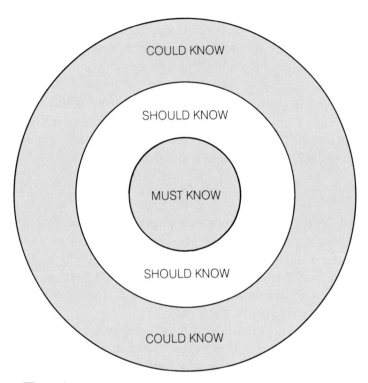

The trainer must keep in mind the students' learning priorities

When writing lesson plans, one important question that should be asked but which is generally overlooked is, 'What is the best way to *learn* this topic?' (Not teach it.)

A session plan should ideally have five columns (refer to the sample shown at the end of this chapter). They should be titled:

- Timing
- Content (what is to be taught)
- Training technique
- Trainee activity
- Aids required.

Timing indicates the running time of the session. It allows the trainer to pace activities throughout the session and finish on time.

Content lists all of the things that have to be covered during the session. Generally, key words are all that are required as memory joggers.

Training technique indicates whether the particular section of the session is to be of a lecture style, show and tell, or perhaps participant discovery.

Trainee activity is a new concept. If the trainer lists the types of things that the participant will be doing during the session (listening, looking, practising, etc) it becomes possible to build in variety in advance.

Aids required is the column for the trainer to note when training aids are required. It is also a good idea to have all of your aids numbered so that should they get mixed up you can put them back into sequence, or flick through them quickly to find the one needed.

Conclusion

A session plan is an essential piece of equipment for the instructor. It serves to guide the lesson in the correct sequence and ensures that all relevant material is covered during the lesson.

It provides a check to see if objectives are being met. It can be checked by others to see if the session plan and objectives are both working in the same direction and not against each other.

It is very important that lesson plans be revised or updated by the trainer. This should be done as soon as the trainer is aware of the need, or when changes in technology occur which affect the specific lesson.

A well prepared session plan helps the trainer to keep the instruction on target

There is no *best* format or style that may be used for a lesson plan. The best one for an instructor to use is one that is easily understood and which can be used effectively in the classroom setting.

Once a lesson plan has been drafted, the best way to be sure you can improve it is to actually use it. It's surprising how many instructors or trainers leave their lesson plans in their folders and do not refer to them during the lesson.

Application example

Assume that you have been given the task of preparing a lesson on the use of a bundy machine to a group of new employees. One of the first things you would probably do is have a look at the machine to become familiar with it. You would also do some research on its operation, the manufacturer, what it is used for and many other things. When enough background information has been collected the task of writing the session plan can begin.

For this exercise we have to make a few assumptions. We will assume that the session is to last no more than fifteen minutes, that you have six participants and that you have at least one bundy machine as a sample.

It is simplest to write a session plan at this stage and then to modify it if necessary when you look back over it. What should the session plan look like after the initial research has been carried out and the information sorted?

The session plan shown on page 60 may be used by any trainer who has some knowledge of a bundy machine. It is easy to understand and can also be used as a reference document before presenting the session.

At the conclusion of the lesson the trainer should modify the session notes if required, making any alterations while the ideas are still fresh. If this machine becomes superseded so do the session plans and new ones must be made to suit the new machine.

Sample session plan   Sheet No. 1

TITLE: ..How to use the bundy machine ....
                    ....
                    ....

WRITTEN BY: ..Authors name .... DATE: ..... Date written .....

OBJECTIVES: ..At the end of this session the participants will be able to: ....
                    ..1) state one reason for using the bundy machine ....
                    ..2) demonstrate the correct use of the bundy machine ....
                    .....located in the workshop ....
                    ..3) state when the bundy machine is used ....
                    ....

SESSION TIME: .... 15 minutes ....

NUMBER OF PARTICIPANTS: .... 6 ...... (up to 10) ....

ENTRY LEVEL: .... new employees ....

AIDS/EQUIPMENT: .... sample bundy machine ....
                    .... 6 bundy cards for each participant ....
                    .... whiteboard and markers ....
                    ....
                    ....
                    ....
                    ....

POTENTIAL FAULTS:... session not to be conducted at ....
                    ... start or finish time of workshop ....

METHOD: ..... show and tell ....
                    ....

				Sheet No. 2
Timing (minutes)	Content (what to be taught)	Training Technique	Trainee Activity	Aids Required
INTRO 0 – 2	Introduction — Topic — Facilitator	Lecture	Listening	W/board
	Link back to previous session			
	Motivator — pay requirement			
BODY 2 – 10	Describe bundy machine and purpose	Lecture	Listening	Sample Machine & cards
	How to use machine	Show & tell	Observation	Sample Machine & cards
	How to fix simple problems	Show & tell	Observation	Sample Machine
		Go to workshop	Practice	Machine & cards
CONCLUSION 10 – 15	Each participant to demonstrate correct use of the bundy in the workshop	Hands-on	Doing/test	Machine & cards
	Questions to group — give one reason for using the bundy — when do you use the bundy	Questions	Answering verbally	
	Link to next session on Pay and Conditions			

Further reading

Craig, Robert, *Training and Development Handbook*, 2nd edn, McGraw-Hill, New York, 1976.

Field, Laurie, *Skilling Australia*, Longman Cheshire, Melbourne, 1990.

Field, Laurie, *Teaching Practical Work at TAFE*, Published by ITATE, Sydney, 1984.

Goad, Tom, *Delivering Effective Training*, University Associates, California, 1982.

Sample session plan   Sheet No. 1

Title _____

_____

_____

Written by _____ Date _____

Objectives _____

_____

_____

_____

_____

_____

_____

_____

Session time _____

Number of participants _____

Entry level _____

Aids/Equipment _____

_____

_____

_____

_____

_____

_____

Potential faults _____

_____

Method _____

_____

	Sample session plan			Sheet No. 2
Timing	Content (what to be taught)	Training technique	Trainee activity	Aids required

CHAPTER 9

Methods of instruction

All trainers must realise that if the same method of instruction is used all the time, it can build a barrier to learning. For example, a trainer who uses games and role plays all the time might have little success with that method when instructing a group in the use of a computer. Similarly, the trainer who uses lecture technique constantly might find that it is sometimes inappropriate or that some variety is needed.

The intention here is to list fifteen different methods of instruction then very briefly describe when or where they can be used effectively. It's important to remember that these methods are not all limited to the classroom. Many of them may be used outdoors. The methods to be discussed here are:

- the lecture
- a modified lecture
- the demonstration
- student practice
- student reading
- group discussion
- a fishbowl
- role-plays
- simulation
- games
- videos/films
- brainstorming
- programmed instruction
- field trips
- question and answer.

Methods

The **lecture** is often referred to as *talking to* or *talking at* the group; it is simply addressing a passive audience. To be effective, lecturers need to be on top of things at all times and to be interesting or amusing to the audience. They also need to use an appropriate number of analogies, use the correct level of language for the audience and use a logical sequence of ideas in the presentation. Many institutions in our education system still use the lecture, but with this method the students cannot contribute to the learning experience. However, one significant advantage of the lecture is that the presentation time can be judged to the minute.

For a lecture to be effective, the presenter needs to be aware of the student at all times. The presenter's voice is particularly important both in level and tone. Also the material must be made meaningful to the group so that they will want to listen. It is also possible, and advisable, to use training aids in a lecture presentation.

Unfortunately, the lecture does not generally allow for any form of immediate evaluation, or for any two-way communication between the presenter and the audience.

The lecture method of training can be very effective as long as the lecturer gives an interesting presentation

A **modified lecture** is similar to a lecture except that the lecturer encourages some group participation. This modified lecture is now very common in adult training; the lecturer often relies on the participants' experiences to generate some form of discussion.

The lecturer/presenter needs to make it clear from the beginning that the session is not a straight lecture and that in fact group discussion or participation is welcomed. Questions should also be encouraged. This form of presentation should allow for some form of evaluation at the end.

The modified lecture is an extremely efficient method of instruction and is commonly used in private training programs. When preparing for this type of presentation you will need to allow sufficient time for group participation.

The **demonstration** allows the students to observe what the presentation is about. Most demonstrations are limited to situations requiring motor skills, such as using a bundy machine or folding a serviette. But this need not be the case. Demonstrations could also be used to show students some of the interpersonal skills, such as interviewing and counselling.

A demonstration should follow a planned sequence: a verbal explanation, showing the item or skill, demonstrating the skill, student questioning and student practice.

Among the things to remember when using demonstrations are that you should break the task into bite-size pieces so that the student can progress through mini-goals rather than trying to achieve everything at once. When demonstrating you must ensure that all members of the group can see the demonstration. It is also a good idea to check that all your equipment is in working order before the demonstration begins (to save embarrassment). Above all, make sure that there is ample time for students to practise the skill.

For further information on skill demonstration refer to Chapter 7.

Student practice should be allowed for after every method of instruction. It is pointless to teach someone a new skill but not encourage them to use and perfect it. It is the trainer's responsibility to encourage trainees to apply the skill. Under supervised practice, students find out whether they can use the new skill effectively or not. The trainer also finds out whether the final objective of the student being able to perform the skill out of the controlled atmosphere of the training room has been reached.

Student practice on-the-job is where we finally observe behavioral changes. This is the most effective form of practice and ultimately the most important evaluation.

Positive feedback to the student from this exercise is also likely to encourage them to want to know more and may encourage them to undertake further instruction in the area. They learn the effectiveness of training.

Student reading can be used effectively or it may be a total waste of everyone's time and effort. Student reading before or during a course can be extremely relevant to group discussions and exercises. However, if there are one or two participants who for some reason did not do the set reading, it may mean that they don't know what's happening if the rest of the group decides to carry on. Alternatively, the group may have to mark time while the trainer brings these people up-to-date with a quick overview.

Students must be given an incentive to spend their own time reading course material. The trainer could perhaps tell them that there will be a quiz for them to do. Also, they should know that if they don't do the required reading they will be wasting not only their time but the time of the group as well. A recent idea is to give the participants note-pads which have structured exercises for them to perform while reading. An example of such exercises could be a series of statements with missing words or phrases that the participant must fill in. If the trainer uses a structured note-pad, many other forms of assignment can be designed for the student to undertake while reading.

Group discussion. This covers many methods of discussion and we will look at three of them briefly.

Structured discussion is a discussion between the participants to meet set objectives. It is usually better for the group to have input into the topics to be covered to meet the objective, as this gives them more motivation. The motivation comes from the fact that they were basically responsible for setting the agenda.

Open-forum discussion, an unstructured discussion, is basically a free-for-all with the facilitator as a go-between or referee. This type of discussion can be used to voice opinions or vent frustrations. One problem that can arise is that the group may have one or two dominant people who tend to do all the talking. The facilitator should set ground rules before the discussion starts (or during it, if necessary). One solution is to nominate an object in the room as the 'microphone'. Only the person holding the microphone may speak, and when it is passed on to someone else the new holder takes a turn.

Panel discussions are almost like a lecture in that they generally do not allow for a great deal of participant input. The panel is usually made up of a group of topic experts each with their own sub-topic. The facilitator starts at a logical point and each expert builds on what the previous expert has said, all of the topics being related. To be effective this instruction method needs to be mixed with a question and answer method, or perhaps the requirement for the participants to do some preliminary work on the subject matter.

For further information on group discussion or group work refer to Chapter 10.

A **fishbowl** is a description for a particular type of exercise. It is a method that can be used for analysis of group process or as a monitor of the effectiveness of group discussion.

The participants need to be seated in two circles, a small inner circle with a larger circle around it. The trainer usually selects an important, or controversial, topic and formulates several discussion-provoking questions. These questions are given to one person in the inner circle. It is the responsibility of those in the inner circle to keep the discussion going on the set topic. A number of observers are appointed to sit in the outer circle and they are asked to note things such as who is doing all the talking, who is interrupting, does the discussion get sidetracked very often, are there many disagreements, are there any signs of nonverbal communication, and any other points the facilitator wants to include in the debriefing of the exercise. The group members should be shuffled around so that all have at least one turn in the inner circle as a participant and a turn in the outer circle as an observer.

This is obviously a fairly complicated method and it would be advisable for new trainers to avoid a fishbowl until they feel comfortable with simpler group work methods.

Role-plays are situational examples. A role-playing exercise normally involves the trainer, or sometimes the group, in designing a simple script about a situation the participant may be placed in. It is then a matter of getting some of the group members to act out the situation in identified positions, using previous experience, new knowledge or skills given to them, or other methods they would like to try under controlled conditions.

Try to let the participants do most of the work, because this will give them the commitment to follow the role-play through. Don't use too many props as they may be distracting; let the group members use their imagination for the setting. Make the whole show fast-moving and try to get everyone involved. Use different players in the same situation for different ideas if needed.

It is essential that a debriefing be held as soon as the role-play exercise is finished. This gives everyone feedback on the process and highlights important points or issues raised by the group.

Simulations are sometimes used for team-building exercises. They are not unlike role-plays but are more complex in their structure and require more participant input. For a simulation, the group has to act in a team role, such as a team of consultants or a board of directors. With large groups it is advisable to break them into smaller teams with different exercises. This requires all of the team members to have an input into the exercise.

The groups are normally placed in a situation where they must get together and solve problems or build empires. It is normally a very descriptive exercise and may run for a number of months.

When the simulations have been completed, let the groups present their findings or results to all the participants. Not only may someone pick up some good ideas, it is a conclusion to the exercise. In some simulations a lot of team effort is used, and this presentation period is the group's opportunity to show how successful they were.

Simulations are also used for the individual trainee. Such exercises tend to be complex and generally expensive to set up. Those involving an individual trainee may be things like flight simulators and driving simulators.

Games can be simple (joining the dots in the shortest time) or very complex (Who can show a million-dollar profit first?). Games are normally competitive and usually relate directly to the task involved.

If games are made to be competitive they should not identify winners and losers, but should identify a variety of thoughts and ideas and show how others may use them.

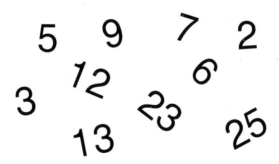

A wide variety of interesting, competitive games can be used in training situations

When games are used to develop or improve skills, they can be used at any stage during the course. Experienced trainers tend to keep their games for use after breaks. If you find a lively game that gets everyone involved and moving around, it may be worth designing your session so that this game can be used immediately after lunch.

There are many books now available that contain hundreds of proven games for different topics. If you design your own games and they are successful, share them with other trainers.

For more information on games, simulations and role-plays see Chapter 1.

Videos or **films** may generally be used as support for the trainer but they should not be used as the sole method of instruction. If trainees have difficulties with the material or have questions to be answered, they need someone to talk to. Videos and films are usually used to reinforce the main points of the trainer's presentation. It may be desirable to use a video or film occasionally as a change of pace.

If videos or films are used to support the trainer they must be introduced to the group and the group be made aware of what to look for. At the conclusion, the trainer must review the ideas and material covered and clarify any points that may not have been understood.

The trainer must preview any video or film before it is used. Check that it is relevant, that it covers the points required, and that it isn't out of date.

A training session should not be designed around the film content; the film should fit into the previously designed session. The film should complement the session.

Brainstorming, a form of structured discussion, is a method of instruction that is not being used to it's full extent. It has the advantage of using the participants' own thoughts and so this leads to more ideas and greater participant motivation.

The trainer must first introduce a topic or problem to the group, then it is up to the participants to give as many ideas or thoughts as possible. All ideas must be positive; no negative ideas allowed. They are listed on a whiteboard or flip chart but not discussed straight away. The object is to get as many ideas as possible and it doesn't matter how absurd they are (ridiculous ideas are encouraged). When the group has been exhausted of ideas then you can go back and start discussing each idea. The group then decides on which ideas are best suited to the problem and applies the results.

Brainstorming with a group gives more, and generally better, ideas than an individual is able to provide. This is called synergy; the total is greater than the sum of the parts.

Programmed instruction (computer-based instruction) is not a new idea, but is now becoming more recognised through the use of computers.

The concept of programmed instruction is to break a task into as many segments as possible. Each segment has to be mastered by the trainees before they are allowed to progress to the next one. If they are unable to answer questions on a section correctly, they are given more exercises to perform until the section has been mastered.

With this method of instruction the trainee must have an input to the learning process. If they don't participate, nothing happens. When the trainees are participating, their efforts are acknowledged, whether they are right or wrong.

Programmed instruction may be used for any topic, from playing chess, to reading skills, to flying a plane. It's easy to see why computers are now being used in programmed instruction, as they can give the trainee more and more exercises, or speed up to suit the faster or more knowledgable learner.

Trainees can proceed at their own pace with programmed instruction

Field trips may be useful if they have been properly thought out. If we intend taking our trainees on some sort of excursion or tour it must be planned.

The trip must be meaningful to the trainees and they must be motivated to want to attend. When we plan our field trip we are designing a complete session. The only difference is that the session isn't being conducted totally in the classroom. The design of the session will include a clearly stated objective, a need for the trainees to be attentive, an introduction to the exercise, a body (the trip itself), a conclusion (or debriefing), and some form of evaluation.

A popular method used for field trips is to give the trainees a number of exercises or observations to be carried out during the trip. This concept can be used for any form of field trip, including visits to other offices.

A well planned field trip, with associated exercises for the trainees, can be a useful training method

Question and answer techniques are employed in most classrooms. This technique can also be called 'modified discussion'. It involves some trainee participation and gives the trainer a good indication of whether the message is being received or not. It may indicate that some areas need to be revised or revisited.

The trainer should ask questions of the group often, making sure that they are relevant to the topic. The questions must be spread around the group so that all of the trainees are participating. If people are having trouble answering the question, don't give them the answer. You can rephrase the question, prompt them, give them clues or get someone else in the group to assist them.

Conclusion

A trainer should not rely on a sole method of instruction for all subjects. The experienced trainer will be able to look at a topic and decide on a number of methods that can be used independently, or combined, for maximum benefit to the learner.

The trainer must make the decision on which method to use based on the learners' requirements, *not* on what the trainer feels like doing. It has been found that most participants want to have some form of input to the learning exercise, so the trainer should consider using the participants' knowledge in the session design and the methods selected.

A well-structured course would have more than one method of instruction in its design. Remember that variety is necessary—but don't go overboard.

Application example

What works for one trainer may not necessarily work for another. As most trainers use different methods of instruction, there will not be an application example for this chapter. However, as an exercise, you can think of a subject that you haven't instructed in before. With this subject in mind, try to see it from the learner's point of view, write down some methods that may get the message across in a non-threatening way. If you can't think of a subject, try something like law or office procedures.

When you have done this, apply the same idea to something you are instructing in now. Are you surprised that you may have seen it differently from the learner's point of view? It may be time to modify some of your session plans to incorporate other methods of instruction.

An interesting session I once participated in was a legal presentation on the area of omission and commission. It started with a group of trainers carrying in a corpse (fake) on a table covered with a sheet. The staff became the main role-players with the audience playing the part of the jury. Without going into great detail I think that you can see that a strong learning atmosphere was created from a relatively boring subject.

The new trainer has to start somewhere, so you will probably use other trainers ideas to begin with. These ideas may or may not be right and they may or may not suit you. Once you have used them you must modify them to suit your own style.

Further reading

Baird, L., Schneier, C. & Laird, D., *The Training and Development Source-book*, Human Resource Press, Massachusetts, 1985, Part 1, Section VI, B.

Goldstein, Irwin, *Training: Program Development and Evaluation*, Brooks/Cole Publishing, California, 1974, Chapter 8.

Laird, Dugan, *Approaches to Training and Development*, Addison-Wesley Publishing Company, Massachusetts, 1978, Chapter 10.

Mill, Cyril, *Activities for Trainers: 50 Useful Designs*, University Associates, California, 1980.

Newstrom, J. W. & Scannell, E. E., *Games Trainers Play*, McGraw-Hill Book Company, New York, 1980.

Poulter, Bruce, *Training and Development*, CCH Australia Ltd, Australia, 1982, Chapter 4.

Scannell, E. E. & Newstrom, J. W., *More Games Trainers Play*, McGraw-Hill Book Company, New York, 1983.

Zemke, R. & Kramlinger, T., *Figuring Things Out: A Trainers Guide to Needs and Task Analysis*, Addison-Wesley Publishing Company, Massachusetts, 1981, Chapter 18.

CHAPTER 10

Group methods

This chapter will look closely at one of the methods of instruction described in the previous chapter. It will deal specifically with the techniques and purposes of group sessions and group work, as used in workshops, as well as seminars and conferences. The main ideas are basically the same regardless of which setting they are used in. We will also be looking at some suggestions for effective use of these methods.

What are group methods?

Group methods describe a number of activities including games, simulations, role-playing, team-building exercises and brainstorming. In group methods we also include some of the group techniques such as the Nominal group process, Dacum, Critical incident technique and the Delphi technique. Group methods can best be described as a process of sharing ideas and roles between individuals in a group setting.

Ideas and roles are the two main issues involved with a group. There must be a leader so that the group is guided to achieve its objective—the task it was brought together for in the first place. However, as well as achieving that objective, the group is involved in the *process* of getting the task done. Ideally there should be a balance between the task and the process.

Historically with new trainers the main concern is getting the group to perform to get the task done. Experienced trainers are more likely to be concerned with how the performance was designed or processed, in addition to the ultimate outcome.

In many group meetings the group leader wants to get something done, but does not care how the outcome is reached. On the other hand, some group leaders can see that the process may be just as important as the outcome. They still get the job done, and tend to get it done more effectively because the group feels motivated to carry it out properly.

What types of groups are there?

As trainers or facilitators we probably deal with five separate types of groups or meetings.

The five are:

- group discussions
- conferences
- seminars
- workshops
- clinics.

There are a number of other types of groups or meetings we could consider, but they tend not to be relevant to training situations. Before we carry on it may be of benefit to look at a quick outline of the five groups.

Group discussions are normally groups of five to twenty people with common interests in the subject area. It is a conversational style of discussion where all of the individual members have equal rights and access to the subject. A group discussion must be under the control of a trained facilitator or group leader. This group leader remains impartial in discussion, but ensures that the group stays on the topic and that all participants do in fact have equal input.

Conferences are usually larger groups. The numbers may vary from five to one hundred or more. The participants normally represent different departments or organisations, but all have a common interest or background.

Some conferences are simply venues for participants to exchange ideas or information

The activity of a conference is usually to look at problems within the specified subject area and endeavour to arrive at solutions to them by the end of the conference time. Some conferences are simply venues for participants to exchange ideas or information, or to find out about new technology in the industry that they represent.

Seminars are groups of any size, from five to five hundred, and they are conducted for a group of people who have a common need. Seminars are normally led by an expert in the topic area. In this form of group method, a problem may be defined and then given to the participants to rectify, under the supervision of the seminar leader. The seminar leader may also present relevant research findings so that the participants can discover the correct solutions based on those findings. Seminars usually follow more of a lecture format.

Seminars usually begin with a presentation by an expert, before small groups form for discussion

Workshops may be groups of any size, but again the group would have a common interest or a common background. A workshop is generally conducted so that the participants can improve their ability or understanding by combining study and discussion. Workshops tend to be user-driven; that is, the participants may influence the direction of the program from its very beginning.

Clinics are meetings where a small group of people with common interests examine a real-life problem. The group members diagnose and analyse the problem and then offer solutions. Clinics may be used to establish procedures, as they are based on real-life situations, and the participants generally offer working solutions based on their past experiences.

What are the group techniques?

Nominal group process involves a group of people who meet to solve a problem described to them by the group leader. In silence and to the clock, the group members must write down a number of their individual responses or ideas. The group leader then takes one idea at a time and lists them all on a chart or board. If explanation or clarification is needed it is provided by the originator of the idea after all of the ideas have been collected from the group. After all the ideas have been listed, the group members must individually rank the responses. The group leader takes these individual rankings and processes them to give the final rankings of the combined group.

One possible problem with this technique is that it doesn't draw on facts. However, this may be offset by the time efficiency of the whole process.

DACUM (Develop A CurriculUM) is normally used by training staff to develop a curriculum, and is achieved by dissecting a position into jobs and tasks. A group of ten to fifteen experts (usually supervisors or skilled workers) sets aside a period of time at a venue free from distractions. The group leader is responsible for having an occupation or position dissected so that a curriculum can be designed to meet the exact training needs of the employee.

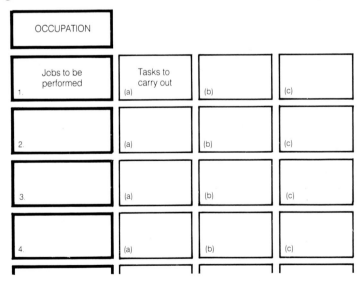

DACUM, one of the group techniques, involves dissecting a position into various jobs and tasks

This technique may also be used to establish varying levels of competency of the employee (that is, basic levels, intermediate levels and advanced levels of knowledge or skill proficiency).

Critical incident technique involves having each individual in a group identify the critical incidents which lead to the problem or situation which has been described. When all of the incidents have been collected, they are collated and then discussed by the group. The individuals in this group must have a common interest or background in the subject matter. This technique is sometimes used in management training to get the participants to identify critical incidents in their career. It may also be used for such things as finding out what critical incidents cause the photocopier to jam up.

Delphi technique is a group technique where the group members don't need to get together. It could be called 'the group you have when you're not having a group'. It works like this: A problem or situation is identified by a management or decision-making team. A group leader is asked to identify a number of experts within the subject area. With these experts identified the group leader develops and distributes a questionnaire based on the problem or situation. When the responses have been processed, the group leader then develops and distributes a second questionnaire modified to suit the previous responses. The second and subsequent questionnaires ask the respondents to reconsider their ideas based on new or composite opinions. The process may finish with the second questionnaire or continue until the group of experts reaches consensus on the suggested outcome. With consensus reached, it is then up to the group leader to report the findings back to the management team.

This technique may be modified for use with an assembled group. If it is your intention to use the group in this manner, it is suggested that a lot more study be carried out on the techniques involved.

Advantages and disadvantages of group techniques

As all of these group techniques have their own advantages and disadvantages (see table), it is possible to identify areas where they may be applied. Trainers may apply all of them in a training needs analysis.

It's not expected that new trainers will be 'thrown in the deep end' without some form of assistance. Should the new trainer be required to facilitate any of these group techniques, they would need to conduct much more research; the information presented here is an overview only.

The success of all group work depends heavily on the amount and quality of planning and preparation carried out in advance. You may find it worthwhile contacting the participants before any group meeting to advise them of the problem or situation. This may lead to additional ideas being generated as they have been given some thinking time beforehand.

Technique	Advantages	Disadvantages
Nominal group	Can create group motivation Everyone participates Incorporates brainstorming Generates ideas Opportunity for discussion	Can easily become boring Cost of not having experts at work Effect on productivity with experts gone Threatening if not enough ideas to list Embarrassment by lack of ideas
DACUM	No room for error Incorporates brainstorming Cost effective Good representation of staff Generates specific information	Time consuming Tense to tiring Needs competent leader Can get bogged down in detail May miss attitudinal changes needed
Critical incident	Directly task related Input from participants Not always negative incidents Establishes correct procedures Looks at the entire situation	Time consuming and cumbersome Defining what is and isn't critical Only critical incidents are recorded Input restricted to memories Needs competent leader
Delphi	Selective participation Geographically unrestricted Respondents are isolated Groups can be large Confidentiality	Long duration Lack of ongoing interest No personal contact Unpredictable response rate Data can be lost

Conclusion

This chapter has provided an overview of the basics of group methods and group techniques, which the new trainer needs to know. Very importantly, there is a *process* within all groups which is not investigated here, and would be considered an advanced level of knowledge for trainers. As new trainers gain experience with groups they will begin to notice these processes, and will then be able to influence the group to move in the desired direction, if needed.

It may be of interest to note that all of the group techniques we have looked at (with the exception of nominal group techniques) stipulate that the participants should have a common interest or background in the subject matter. If this common interest is missing, you may find it almost impossible to reach your objectives. However, in a nominal group process it isn't necessary for the individuals to have a common interest or background in the subject matter because the aim might be to find new ideas or solutions. Someone without an in-depth knowledge of the problem or situation may be able to offer the best solution based on their outside expertise or ideas.

Application example

An application example wouldn't be practical for this chapter, so instead I will give you some tips for starting and maintaining group discussion:

- Select a topic that everyone can become involved in.
- Let the group set ground rules for everyone to follow.
- Acknowledge all input from the participants.
- Select as your first speaker the one who will give a model answer.
- Go around the circle to begin with.
- Don't leave the expected worst responses to last.
- Ensure that everyone gets a chance to participate.
- Always get clarification if needed.
- Look for nonverbal responses.
- Use first names and direct eye contact with the group.
- Don't always give the answers; let the group do it.
- Plant seeds so that the group may develop their own ideas.
- Move from the foreground to the background as the discussion proceeds.
- Intervene if necessary and keep the group on track.
- Be aware of your nonverbal communication.
- Be honest and enthusiastic with the group at all times. If you're not, you can bet they won't be.

Further reading

Craig, Robert, *Training and Development Handbook*, 2nd edn, McGraw-Hill Book Company, New York, 1976, Chapter 34.

Daniels, William, *Group Power: A Manager's Guide to Using Meetings*, University Associates, California, 1986.

Dimock, Hedley, *Groups: Leadership and Group Development*, University Associates, California, 1987.

Hanson, Philip, *Learning through Groups: A Trainer's Basic Guide*, University Associates, California, 1981.

Laird, Dugan, *Approaches to Training and Development*, Addison-Wesley Publishing Company, Massachusetts, 1978, Chapter 10.

CHAPTER 11

Games, simulations and role-plays

We have all seen and probably participated in training games simulations and role-plays. Just because we are aware of them, does this mean that we can use them anytime we feel like it? No, it doesn't.

What we will be doing now is looking at the differences between games, simulations and role-plays. We will consider when it may be appropriate to use them and we will look at a brief example of each.

The use of games, simulations and role-plays allows the participant to *discover* outcomes, rather than being told everything without trying it. Most of the world's airlines, manufacturing plants, human resource companies, military establishments, small and large companies, private and public organisations now use games, simulations and role-plays in training. The ultimate outcome of using games, simulations and role-plays is improved learning.

What is the difference?

A game

A game is an activity, illustration or exercise that can support the point the trainer is trying to get across to the trainees. A game is normally brief, is

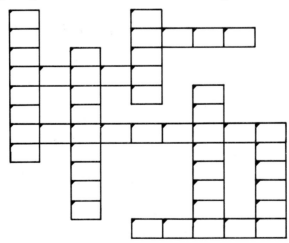

The use of games in training helps the participants to discover the outcome of actions for themselves

not felt as threatening by the participants, requires all the participants to participate, is not complicated, is inexpensive, generally contains one learning point, is predictable in its results and is generally adaptable to a wide variety of situations.

A game may not always appear to have any direct relevance to the topic. The participant may not see the relevance or the point the trainer wanted to make until the experience is discussed later. If this discussion does not take place the trainee may never see the connection between the game and the subject matter, and the whole exercise is wasted.

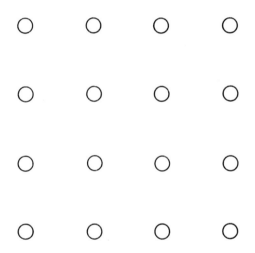

Can you join the 16 dots with six straight continuous lines?
(You are not allowed to lift your pencil off the paper or retrace your path.)

Games are an ideal way to provide activity, but their contribution to learning must be made clear too

A simulation

A simulation is usually more complex than a game in its design. Simulations are the trainer's mock-up of the real thing. They can range from a simple paper mock-up of utensils or furniture, to exact replicas of the inside of a motor vehicle or aircraft using sophisticated computers to run them. The cost of these simulators can range from a few dollars to many millions of dollars. Even if they only cost a couple of dollars though, you will generally find that they require a lot of trainer preparation time.

The use of a simulation allows the participant to try new behaviours without endangering the real product or suffering terrible consequences if something goes wrong.

Simulation exercises can be very instructive

A role-play

A role-play is similar to a simulation except that it doesn't use any props. Normally the only items required for a role-play are a script, or an idea, and one or more participants. The situations that the participants act out are usually related to the workplace and involve situations that the players might be involved in. After the role-players have been identified they act out the parts as they would normally, or perhaps try new behaviours shown to them during training. After the scenario has been played out, the role-players, the rest of the group and the trainer carry out a critique of the role-play. They identify good and bad points, include suggestions for other behaviours and suggest any other possibilities.

Role-plays are normally followed by group discussion, and time must be allowed for this very important part of the session.

Role-playing is a vivid way of learning how to handle on-the-job situations

When can we use these techniques?

For most of us, games, simulations and role-plays were part of the process of growing up. Right back to our earliest recollections of school days, we remember playing games such as marbles or hide-and-go-seek. It is now recognised that these games are not only for fun, but also prepare the child for entry into the social system. If any of you took Home Economics, Woodwork or Metalwork at school you would probably call them simulations of the real workplace. Some of us may also remember when we acted out roles in a game of 'Mothers and Fathers'—another form of role-play. We can actually trace the use of games and simulations back thousands of years. Chess is an example of this. It was developed by the military and was based on solving military problems.

In a training situation we must be very selective in the use and timing of these methods of instruction. People become bored doing the same thing all the time, even if it is a 'mind-blowing' experience the first few times. If you intend using these methods effectively, plan them into your session notes or outline. This is one situation where we definitely need to apply the principles of adult learning. (Review the nine principles in Chapter 1.)

So when can you use them? They may be used any time as long as you feel that using a game, simulation or role-play would be the most effective way for the participants to learn what they are intended to learn or discover. Don't just use them for the sake of variety.

You can, however, use games, or drills, as a means of channelling excess energy or to liven up the class. The activity can be a means of improving the learning atmosphere. So games or drills should be selected and used on the basis of their usefulness, for reinforcing the instruction, or improving the learning environment.

Samples

A game

A simple type of game for part of a trainer training course might be to see who can draw the straightest line on the whiteboard, the winner receiving a new whiteboard marker. This type of game is simple, non-threatening, has no losers and is inexpensive.

Discussion later would highlight the main purpose behind the game. This might be to let the trainees see that it's not as easy as it looks to draw that line on the whiteboard. The game could also motivate some of the trainees to improve their techniques on the whiteboard through practice.

A simulation

We have probably all seen a tennis serving machine. If you haven't, it's a machine which is set up on one side of a tennis court and 'serves' tennis balls out at different speeds and angles. Wouldn't you agree that this is a simulation? Wouldn't you also agree that using this serving machine is easier to organise than trying to get a group of tennis players for your trainee to practice with? Using this type of equipment would also allow for a greater variation of 'players' anyway.

After the training session using the machine, we would have a debriefing period which would give suggestions to improve bad returns. If the trainee encounters a large number of bad returns, they won't continuously lose the game using this type of simulation. Imagine how hard it would be to want to try to improve yourself if you kept on losing 'real' matches.

A role-play

If we were training welfare workers, wouldn't it be fair to assume that we would want them to counsel someone as part of their training? Of course we would. Wouldn't it be also fair to assume that we couldn't just go out onto the street to find volunteers? Right again. This is where the role-play comes in. We would probably describe a scenario to the group and then ask a couple of the participants to come forward and act it out. After they had completed that task, and we had discussed the effects, we could then break the group into smaller groups and get all of them to role-play other similar situations. The concluding discussion should involve ideas for improvements, based on the role-playing experience.

Conclusion

Gone are the days when games and the like were not considered to be suitable training methods. Training is a serious business, but we can and should use games or simulations in training.

War games (simulations) have been used by military personnel for many, many centuries and have proved to be very effective. Games, simulations and role-plays are relatively new to training, and they are also proving to be very effective, if used properly.

Regardless of how good we are as presenters or lecturers, we can't fool ourselves into thinking that our presentation alone is going to keep everyone's interest for the whole period. The use of a game or simulation is an application of the principles of adult learning. Be sure that the participants do not become over-involved in the game or simulation and so actually miss the learning point. Also, if the participants have too high a level of enthusiasm for the game or simulation, they may become bored with normal training.

The learning process can be speeded up by the use of games, simulations and roleplays. It's well known that people learn better when they are enjoying themselves. So we should think seriously about creating or supplying the appropriate learning atmosphere.

We should always select the training method *after* we have set the objectives, and it should respond to the trainees' needs, not the trainer's.

When we decide to start using a game, simulation or role-play it is important that we practise the exercise at least once with a group of people not involved in the immediate presentation. This helps the trainer to see if the design is going to work, and in the expected way. Like all types of training, games, simulations and role-plays must be evaluated for their worth and effectiveness. If they don't produce what is needed, scrap or modify them.

Application example

An application example for this chapter would serve little purpose. All it would do is give you another example of a game, simulation or role-play.

What I would suggest now is that you read about a number of games, simulations and role-plays. Three of the texts listed at the end of this chapter contain hundreds of examples. The texts are:

The inventive trainer can design new forms of familiar games to provide variety

- *100 Training Games*
- *Activities for Trainers: 50 Useful Designs*
- *Games Trainers Play.*

Read as many texts as you feel comfortable with; these three are fun. Use your imagination to see where you could use them. When we talk about designing new games or simulations, it's normally a matter of modifying an existing design to suit new conditions. Totally new games or simulations are very rare.

Further reading

Bourner, Tom, Martin, Vivien & Race, Phil, *Workshops that Work*, McGraw-Hill Book Company, London, 1993.

Christopher, Elizabeth & Smith, Larry, *Leadership: Training Through Gaming*, Nichols Publishing Company, New York, 1987.

Craig, Roben, *Training and Development Handbook*, 2nd edn, McGraw-Hill Book Company, New York, 1976, Chapter 40.

Elgood, Chris, *Handbook of Management Games*, 4th edn, Gower Publishing Company, England, 1988.

Forbess-Greene, Sue, *The Encyclopedia of Icebreakers*, University Associates, California, 1983.

Jones, Ken, *Imaginative Events for Training*, McGraw-Hill Book Company, New York, 1993.

Kroehnert, Gary, *100 Training Games*, McGraw-Hill Book Company, Sydney, 1991.

Mill, Cyril, *Activities for Trainers: 50 Useful Designs*, University Associates, California, 1980.

Morris, Kenneth & Cinnamon, Kenneth, *A Handbook of Non-verbal Group Exercises*, Applied Skills Press, California, 1983.

Morris, Kenneth & Cinnamon, Kenneth, *A Handbook of Verbal Group Exercises*, Applied Skills Press, California, 1983.

Newstrom, J. W. & Scannell, E. E., *Games Trainers Play*, McGraw-Hill Book Company, New York, 1980.

Newstrom, J. W. & Scannell, E. E., *Still More Games Trainers Play*, McGraw-Hill Book Company, New York, 1991.

Newstrom, J. W. & Scannell, E. E., *Even More Games Trainers Play*, McGraw-Hill Book Company, New York, 1994.

Nilson, Carolyn, *Team Games for Trainers*, McGraw-Hill Book Company, New York, 1993.

Rogers, Jennifer, *Adults Learning*, 2nd edn, Open University Press, England, 1979, Chapter 8.

Scannell, E. E. & Newstrom, J. W., *More Games Trainers Play*, McGraw-Hill Book Company, New York, 1983.

Van Ments, Morry, *The Effective Use of Role-Play*, Kogan Page Ltd, London, 1987.

CHAPTER 12

Measuring trainee achievement

What is trainee achievement?

When we talk about measuring trainee achievement we are concerning ourselves with a number of issues. Trainee achievement seems to mean something like 'has the trainee achieved the course objectives?'. But is this what it's all about? To put it simply, *no*.

It's true that we are interested in measuring results to see if the trainee has developed a change in behavior or attitude. But questions such as 'was the training cost effective?' and 'is the organisation now better equipped?' are finally the most important ones.

Whatever the reason for measuring trainee achievement, it has to be done. Even though most trainers know this, very few do it.

Before we look at the process, we need to define the difference between measurement and evaluation. The term 'measurement' indicates the things that we can observe and count. Measurement should be directly related to the things that were measured during the training needs analysis. It is simply the collection of relevant data. The term 'evaluation' indicates the assumptions or judgments we make from the results of the measurement. If that measurement is the same system as that used during the training needs analysis, we can then see (evaluate) whether training has been effective.

Consider the following example: Two swimming coaches are talking to each other. One says to the other, 'Things are certainly getting better. I had six fewer people drown on my courses this year; that's a big improvement'. By looking at this statement we can say that the *measurement* is the fact that the coach had six fewer people drown this year. The *evaluation* is the part of the statement that says things are getting better and that things are improving. These are the judgments made from the measurements.

In Chapter 2 we looked at training gaps. By measuring trainee achievement we are trying to establish whether such gaps have been filled or not, and that makes a lot of sense.

Some of the things that we may measure both before and after training are:

- cost of rejects
- cost of wasted materials
- turnover of staff
- number of industrial disputes
- number of accidents
- absentee rates
- amount of unfinished work
- number of equipment breakdowns
- number of sales calls made.

This list could go on and on, but the point is that the trainer needs to have relevant information before training, and relevant information after training. With this information or data (measurement) we can assess (evaluate) the effectiveness of the training and perhaps modify the training to suit the results. If the evaluation shows no improvement, the training should be dropped.

Trainee achievement can be measured or tested in many ways. Chapter 19 will deal with these methods.

When to take measurements

Measurements or testing should be carried out at four different stages. The first measurement should be made when we do our training needs analysis. After all we did need to establish that we had a need, and we had to prove that need, didn't we? The trainer should have decided what to measure to prove this need.

The second measurement is normally taken during the training process. This data tells us if we are meeting our mini-goals during training, indicating whether the session objectives are being met.

Our third measurement is made at the immediate conclusion of the training programme. This is typically a pen-and-paper test or the practical demonstration of a task. It's interesting to note that the collection of data finishes here in most cases.

The fourth measurement should be collected when the formal training is over and the former trainee is back at the workplace. It's impossible to effectively evaluate a course on 'Safety in the Workplace' without a measurement of how many fewer accidents have occurred in the workplace since training was undertaken.

It's important to note that the item decided upon as the relevant one for measurement must be identified before any data is collected. Once the item to be measured is decided on, we must stick to it. There is no point in measuring the cost of labour to wash cars before the operators are trained to do it efficiently, and then, on conclusion of the training, finding out whether the cars are cleaner than they were before training.

As part of this planning we should decide when we are going to take the measurements. With all of this information we can start to develop an action plan. It can now be seen that most of our time will be taken up with the collection of the data rather than its evaluation.

How can we express the results?

When we have evaluated the measurements we can express the results in some kind of report. However, sometimes this might not seem to be conclusive evidence to the groups that need to know. A summary of the results expressed, say, as a percentage of training effectiveness might help. We could say that at the conclusion of the course the training had been 91.1 per cent effective. But how do we get this percentage?

We determine that we have a set number of objectives for a course; let's say eighteen for this course. We then need to know how many participants there were; we will assume that ten people attended. We also need to know how many objectives each participant had met. To find this out, it is necessary to keep a record of trainee achievement during the course. A sample is shown below.

	Trainee									
	1	2	3	4	5	6	7	8	9	10
Objective # 1	✔	✔	✔	✔	✔	✗	✔	✔	✔	✔
Objective # 2	✔	✔	✔	✔	✔	✔	✔	✔	✔	✔
Objective # 3	✗	✔	✔	✔	✔	✔	✔	✔	✔	✔
Objective # 4	✔	✔	✔	✔	✔	✔	✔	✔	✔	✔
Objective # 5	✔	✔	✔	✔	✔	✔	✔	✔	✔	✔
Objective # 6	✔	✔	✔	✔	✔	✗	✔	✔	✔	✔
Objective # 7	✔	✔	✗	✔	✗	✗	✔	✗	✗	✗
Objective # 8	✔	✔	✔	✔	✔	✔	✔	✔	✔	✔
Objective # 9	✔	✗	✔	✔	✔	✔	✔	✔	✔	✔
Objective # 10	✔	✔	✔	✔	✔	✔	✔	✔	✔	✔
Objective # 11	✔	✔	✔	✔	✔	✔	✔	✔	✔	✔
Objective # 12	✔	✔	✔	✔	✔	✗	✔	✔	✔	✔
Objective # 13	✔	✔	✔	✔	✔	✔	✗	✔	✔	✔
Objective # 14	✔	✔	✔	✔	✔	✔	✔	✔	✔	✔
Objective # 15	✔	✔	✔	✔	✔	✔	✔	✔	✔	✗
Objective # 16	✔	✔	✗	✔	✔	✔	✔	✔	✔	✔
Objective # 17	✔	✔	✔	✔	✔	✗	✔	✔	✔	✔
Objective # 18	✔	✔	✔	✔	✔	✔	✔	✗	✔	✔

With this information we can use the following formula:

Number of objectives reached by trainees				
_____	X	$\dfrac{100}{1}$	=	Percentage
Number of objectives that may have been reached by trainees				

$\dfrac{164}{180}$	X	$\dfrac{100}{1}$	=	91.1%

Therefore we can state that this training has been 91.1 per cent effective at the end of the training course. We would expect this percentage to reduce by around 10 to 20 per cent back on the job, but this would depend on many factors. These would be tested separately.

By being able to state our effectiveness as a percentage, we are presenting a professional appearance.

Who is interested in the results?

We can identify at least four interested parties who would want to know the results. The first would be the trainees themselves. After all the time and effort they have put into the training program, they want a measure of their achievement. Remember the nine principles of learning?

Secondly, trainers want to know if they have been successful in filling the training gap.

Thirdly, the trainee's supervisor wants to know if the training has been successful. It may save them time and worry.

And finally, the management wants to know if the training has solved the initial problem, and if it has been cost effective. (Will the end result of this training save money in the long run?)

Conclusion

We can see that the measurement of trainee achievement is a time-consuming process, and we must allow for a percentage of course funds to cover this generally forgotten cost.

Trainers should be prepared to present a well organised report on training results

Measuring trainee achievements (or non-achievements) can be carried out at a number of times before, during and after training. We have identified four common places. Try to use these four as a standard and then improve on them.

Sometimes it may be suggested to you that you should be using control groups and experimental groups to validate your training programme. In most cases, though, the training doesn't need that scale of validation. The important issue is that the problem has been solved or the gap has been filled.

The evaluation is to find out whether the training has filled the training gaps that we originally identified in our training needs analysis.

Application example

Let's assume that a training needs analysis has been carried out and that you've been given the task of training some trainers for an organisation. It would be fair to say that the number of trained, competent trainers had been tested and counted (measured) in the company (the criteria for 'competent' had been clearly defined).

The information collected during the training needs analysis would determine the entry level of the participant to your course. During your course you would be constantly measuring trainee achievement to ensure that the participants were meeting all of the session objectives.

At the end of the training course you would have some form of scale to measure trainee achievement. This scale would be comparable to the scale used in the training needs analysis, to allow comparison and therefore an evaluation (judgment) of how effective the training had been.

Some time after the training had concluded you would again survey the organisation to ascertain that your identified training gap had been filled. You would still need to use the original criteria set in the training needs analysis to establish that the organisation now had enough trained, competent trainers.

When this evaluation has been finalised, the information should be handed to management to show them how effective the training had been. We all recognize that the management report is important, but so is the participant's report. Make sure that participants see the results as well.

It is important that a final check of trainee achievement back on the job is made, as only then can we state that the participants are applying their new knowledge. The end-of-course evaluation tells us that the participants *can* apply this new knowledge, but at that stage we don't know if they *will*.

Further reading

Craig, Robert, *Training and Development Handbook*, 2nd edn, McGraw-Hill Book Company, New York, 1976, Chapter 18.

Goad, Tom, *Delivering Effective Training*, University Associates, California, 1982, Chapter 13.

Goldstein, Irwin, *Training: Program Development and Evaluation,* Brooks/Cole Publishing, California, 1974, Chapters 4 & 5.

Hamblin, A. C., *Evaluation and Control of Training*, McGraw-Hill Book Company, London, 1974.

Mager, Robert, *Measuring Instructional Results*, 2nd edn, Pitman Learning Company, California, 1984.

CHAPTER 13

Trainer effectiveness

This chapter will deal with trainer effectiveness or what we should look for in a good trainer. Fortunately all trainers are not the same as each other, so this chapter is looking at a base level of skills which the new trainer can develop and build on.

The trainer's appearance

A trainer should look like a professional. But how is that achieved? Firstly, the trainer should dress according to the type of instruction being given, and who it's being given to. If you are going to instruct resuscitation techniques to swimmers at a swimming pool, you could safely assume that you don't have to wear your Sunday best. On the other hand, if you're going to instruct a group of senior managers in resuscitation techniques in a board room, you certainly wouldn't be wearing shorts, singlet and sneakers. Ideally, you shouldn't stand out from the crowd, but you should keep your dress standards higher than the rest of the group.

A trainer should also look organised. If you're going into a classroom, have all your material in a neat and organised pile, with the things you want to use first on top, and then work down into the stack.

Have you ever noticed how most trainers carry everything they could ever possibly need, but use only a small percentage of it? If you're going to carry all this material, at least have it organised so that you can find things quickly.

Where should a trainer stand?

If you are going to stand as you present the session, you should be standing in front of the group (looks a bit silly standing at the back). However, if you stand too still you can lose the group's attention, so move around a little, not too much, just enough to keep the participants watching you.

Don't try to hide yourself behind the chair, desk, lectern or overhead projector. This can create a barrier to your communication and therefore to learning. Stand in front or to the side of any equipment, so that the participants can see all of you if they want to.

If you do stand in front of your training aids you must ensure that everyone in the group can see around you. If they can't, your body has become a physical and mental barrier to learning. Also, they may not let you know that you are obscuring their view, it is up to you to notice.

If you're sitting in front of the group, the same principles apply. Allow the group to see all of you. It shows the group that you're open to them and not hiding anything from them.

Communicating with trainees

A lot has been said over the years about trainers' mannerisms. Some of these mannerisms may be verbal ones, such as 'umm', 'errh' and 'you know'. Other types of mannerisms may be rubbing a nose, scratching a neck, fiddling with pens, looking constantly at notes, or trying to crush a whiteboard marker.

If a trainer is using many different types of instructional methods their mannerisms probably aren't too distracting. It's normally only if a trainer spends a long period of time with a group, that any mannerisms need to be thought about and a remedy found. Usually, the more training experience we have, the fewer our distracting mannerisms.

A good trainer can read the trainees' body language. By looking at the participants' faces you can usually tell if they do not understand what the instruction is about. You must also be aware that the trainees can read *your* body language, so don't stand in front of the group with your arms folded and tell them that you're open to questions (unless you want to go home early).

It's important for the trainer not to interrupt a trainee who is talking. A trainee who is cut off may tend to keep quiet after that insult. Obviously there are times when you do have to cut short a trainee who talks too much. If you don't, it can interfere with your communication to the whole group.

For effective communication to continue, the trainer must offer positive reinforcement to the participants during the session. This means acknowledging responses from the group to encourage more interaction. If you ignore any responses, you are likely to lose interaction. Sometimes a particular member may stop contributing after being ignored, even if they have the information you're after.

Trainers must be lively, enthusiastic and full of vitality. If we can display these qualities, it motivates the group to want to learn. If the trainee is not motivated or interested in the instruction, learning may be very difficult, if not impossible.

Communication does not have to mean verbal communication one hundred per cent of the time. Silent pauses during the instruction allow the main points to sink in. So you could plan to have some silent breaks during instruction immediately after the main points.

How should a trainer gain attention?

Humour may be used occasionally to gain the students' attention. When humour is used, the trainer must be certain that it is effective and appropriate. Have you seen a trainer try to use humour to gain attention but lose the group's interest with a joke that didn't quite work?

The trainer must make certain that the topic of the joke is relevant to the training topic, and that the story is not too long as this can distract the participants. Humour must never be directed at any of the trainees, must never use religion, must not refer to any nationality and must never be directed specifically at one sex. These censorship rules ensure that no one in the group is offended. If you offend one person in the class, the whole group may close ranks against you.

To gain, and keep, the trainees' attention we need to use a variety of methods in our instruction. This means that we should use appropriate and relevant training aids where they fit into the session. We must also keep the trainees active and involved in the session (refer to Chapter 9).

Trainers should vary the pitch of their voice occasionally, and volume and pace, to keep the trainees' attention.

By asking questions of the group we can be reasonably certain that we are gaining the participants' attention. If questions are being asked no one wants to be the one who doesn't know the answer, so use it to your advantage.

With this motivating technique we need to follow a few rules. Keep the questions short and spread them around the group. Use 'overhead' type questions. That is, ask a question of the group, wait for a few seconds, and then nominate the participant who is to answer. This technique is sometimes referred to as the 'pose, pause and pounce' method of questioning. Remember to give the trainee praise for a correct answer. If you get an incorrect answer, get the group to help bring out the right answer.

Creating interest

If visual aids are made by the trainer they must be made to attract, and keep, the trainees' interest. When you put notes or phrases on overhead transparencies or on the whiteboard you should make them *mean* something.

By writing legibly and neatly on the whiteboard you can keep the trainees' interest. If the writing is untidy or difficult to understand the trainees may just give up. If you're an untidy writer on the whiteboard, chalkboard or flip chart, take some time to practise so that you improve your style.

To create interest you can always link new material back to something the trainees are familiar with; relating new knowledge to previous knowledge.

Wherever possible, trainers should show that all of the subject matter relates to real life situations. If trainees can see that the information may be of benefit to them, the trainer is creating interest.

A couple of other things that will make it more interesting for the trainees are the use of curiosity and the use of competition. It may be difficult to make the trainees curious about your subject, but think about it and then try it. A sense of competition may also provoke interest, but the trainees should not be in direct competition with each other. They should be competing with themselves by trying to improve on their own previous performance.

Good habits

Good trainers should clean up as they go. Before moving on to a new area in the session, clean the whiteboard of old material and remove any other distractions such as samples or other training aids. Clean up the classroom before leaving, too. This will gain you some professional respect from the trainers in following sessions.

A good trainer should also start and finish on time. How do you feel when you're sitting in a classroom fifteen minutes after the session was supposed to start and the instructor hasn't shown up? How do you feel when the session is still in progress as your train is pulling out of the station?

A good trainer is also thoroughly prepared. This means having your objectives clearly stated, having the appropriate training methods selected, having a session plan and training aids prepared, and knowing where the spares are if anything burns out.

Conclusion

A well-prepared trainer can increase the learning success rate for the trainee if they think a little about it. By looking at yourself from the trainees' point of view, you may wish to change a few things.

Look at your physical appearance. Do you look like a professional educator? Think about where you're standing when you're in front of the group. Can everyone see you? Can everyone see your training aids? Do you look approachable or do you look threatening?

You must be enthusiastic about your material. If you're not enthusiastic about it the trainees certainly won't be. Make the communication two-way and continuous. Reward your trainees when they get it right.

Vary your methods of instruction to keep the participants interested. You need to be continually observing your trainees, ready to regain their attention should it start to wander off.

Your participants won't learn just by being exposed to information. It's up to you as a professional trainer to encourage active learning and to create a learning atmosphere.

Application example

If you think back to the many training sessions you have been involved in as a participant, which do you recall? We all tend to recall the very good presentations and the very bad ones. This tells us as trainers that if we leave a lasting impression on our trainees it will be because we fell into one of these categories. Presumably, you would choose to make that the 'very good' category.

As you recall the best presentation you've sat in on, on the following page write down all the things you liked about it. When you've finished that list, write down all the bad things that you remember about the poorest presentation you have seen. (You may need to think back to school days.)

You can now use this list of good and bad points as a model and guide. The new trainer needs to start somewhere, so why not start with the best?

You will find that if you apply the good points on this list, you're certain to improve your style quite dramatically. If you ignore them, it may take a while for you to get from the bad side to the good side. Even experienced trainers need to sit down and look at their styles occasionally. It is easy to slip back into some bad habits and the trainees generally don't tell us, do they?

Good trainers are/do	Bad trainers are/do

Further reading

Baird, L., Schneier, C. & Laird, D., *The Training and Development Source-book*, Human Resource Press, Massachusetts, 1985, Part 2, Section VI.

Laird, Dugan, *Approaches to Training and Development*, Addison-Wesley Publishing Company, Massachusetts, 1978, Chapter 11.

There hasn't been a great deal written specifically on this subject. Most training and development books have some material scattered through them, so keep your eyes open.

CHAPTER 14

Questioning

Questions are used constantly; without them we would have very little communication. When we think about it, nearly half of what we say or use in general conversation is a question. We pose a question and get a response, then another question is directed at us and we respond, and so on.

This chapter will be looking at the types of questions we use in training. As you read it, you will probably find that the information ties in with your knowledge of questions from everyday conversation.

I have no answers, only questions.

Socrates c. 300 BC

Why do we use questions?

There are many reasons for trainers using questions in a training situation. Most of the reasons are covered in this book but they are mixed through the readings. To make it easier let's list main reasons:

- to find out if there is a training need
- to find the entry level of participants
- to check participant recall
- to find facts
- to assist retention
- to create overlearning
- to involve the participants
- to create active learning
- to gain feedback
- to solve problems
- to check understanding
- to clarify relationships
- to use for revision
- to create discussion
- to keep participants interested
- to stimulate thought
- to re-direct discussion
- to draw on participant experience.

Trainers who don't use questions are missing out on lots of information and assistance. Without the use of questions they risk failure from the very beginning.

Types of questions

Types of questions can be grouped into separate categories. We will now look at the main categories briefly and see where each may be used.

Direct questions are questions that are posed to a certain person in the group. They're not ambiguous and are usually designed to bring out facts. The major problem when using this technique constantly is that it requires only one person to think of a response.

'Fred, what are the nine principles of learning?'

Such questions may be used to check an individual's understanding of the subject matter. Additionally, they may be used to re-direct the group if discussion becomes side-tracked, or to get a day-dreamer involved in the learning process.

Overhead questions are questions that we pose to the whole group, without directing the question at anyone in particular.

'How can we apply this technique in the workplace?' (directed at the whole group).

Overhead questions are used to check group understanding. If no-one in the group volunteers an answer, you may have to rephrase the question or give a clue to the answer.

Alternatively, you can change the question into a direct question by nominating someone to answer it, using the pose, pause and pounce technique.

'How can we apply this technique in the workplace?' (pause) 'Fred?'

This type of questioning is probably the most effective for new trainers to use.

Closed questions usually require a yes/no answer or a single word response. They're quick, but don't give much accuracy if the trainer wants to check knowledge. If you use closed questions, it's sometimes advisable to follow them with a 'what?', 'when?', 'who?', 'where?' or 'how?' to check the trainees' knowledge further.

Trainer: 'Should we always use sessions plans?'

Trainee: 'Yes'

Trainer: 'How?'

Leading questions may be used to get explicit answers. Generally a full description of the situation is given, followed by a question on the subject matter. This question can also include a clue to the answer.

'Let's imagine that you're standing in front of a class and they all appear to be restless. Which of the nine principles of learning could you apply to settle the group down? The nine principles are still shown on the whiteboard.'

This type of question calls for a very specific answer. It may be used as a direct or overhead question and it should be thought provoking, to check the participants' understanding of the material.

Rhetorical questions are questions that don't require answers. What good is a question without an answer? Rhetorical questions are normally used to get the trainees thinking. It's not uncommon for trainers to begin their session by posing a rhetorical question to the group.

'What is testing?'

When you pose a rhetorical question to a group, don't pause too long after it or someone will start to answer, and that defeats the purpose. The purpose of a rhetorical question is to get the group thinking about the subject matter.

Open-ended questions request more information of the trainee and they normally require more time to answer. They usually start with a 'what, when, who, where or how'. Try to avoid questions starting with 'why'. 'Why' questions tend to be too broad in their interpretation. It is commonly accepted that the 'why' is an umbrella for the more specific 'what, when, who, where or how'.

'What do you feel is necessary to accomplish this?'

The answers to open-ended questions may show that the trainer needs to jump in quickly to re-direct the response to the required area of thinking. Sometimes open-ended questions can be used to start group discussion.

Effective questions

A good question should be designed with the following in mind:

- it should be short
- it should have only one idea
- it should be relevant to the topic
- it should create interest
- it should use language that everyone can understand

- it should require more than a guess to answer
- it should be used to emphasise key points
- it should relate to previous knowledge
- it should be a check of knowledge or understanding.

If you ask a question of the individual or the group, make sure that you know what the correct answer is.

When you get a response from a trainee it's a good idea to repeat the answer so that the rest of the group can hear the correct answer. Don't assume that just because you heard the response that everyone else did. Even if they did hear it, repetition provides over-learning.

When posing a question look around the group, not at anyone in particular. If you look at one person it's an indication to everyone that the person you are looking at has been singled out to answer the question.

When you get an incorrect reply don't damage the person's self respect by saying 'No', 'Wrong', 'Stupid', or, my favourite, 'Once again for the dummies'. What you should do is acknowledge the reply, and then prompt the person for the right answer by giving clues or suggestions. Alternatively, you can pass the question to the group for discussion.

All questions should be designed before the session. They should be written on your session plan so that they are not overlooked or forgotten. They will also assist anyone else who uses your session notes.

Conclusion

Questions are an important part of trainer effectiveness. Without questions we would have little, if any, communication. Questions give the trainer feedback on both their own effectiveness and on the level of learning and understanding. They also give trainees an indication of their relative performance.

When we design our session notes we should design the questions at the same time. They should be simple, straightforward questions, not trick questions or questions to show how smart we are. Neither should they be used just to fill in time.

We often use questions to find out if the trainee can relate the new material to previously-known material. Never use questions as punishment.

When you get answers make certain that you acknowledge the participant. If you neglect to do this the participants may withdraw their attention.

Questions may be designed to involve the quiet ones in the group so have some easy questions planned. By getting these right self-confidence is built and this leads to greater participation.

If a question is asked of you by a participant, try to get the group to answer it. This keeps them on their toes and thinking. If the group can't answer the question, try to re-word it so that it can be answered by someone in the group. Give them dues or prompt them in the right direction. Make every effort to get the answer from the group. Rather than *tell* the individual or group, *ask* them.

Application example

As questioning style and techniques vary from trainer to trainer, it's difficult to give an example of how to design and use questions. It is important to remember that we are all different and that what works for one may not work for another. New trainers need to develop their own style of questioning.

Let's look at a training session on questioning. The trainer walks into the room, sits down and poses the question, 'What is a question?' Before anyone in the group answers, the trainer starts the presentation. Posing this question has, the trainer hopes, started the group thinking.

As each important point in the presentation is reached, the trainer asks specific overhead-direct questions. 'What can we do if nobody in the group can answer our question?' (pause) 'Fred, can you tell us?'

At the end of the session the trainer generally asks a few preset questions that relate directly to the session objectives. 'What are ten points that we have to consider whenwe are designing a question?' 'One point each please. Wilma can you give me one?'

Of course all of these questions were designed before the training took place. When they were designed they were included in the session plan so that they wouldn't be forgotten or overlooked.

Remember that we need to test at the end of a session to see if we have met our session objectives; by using questions we can find this out easily and quickly. Using questions is also a method of over-learning. Questions can be our conclusion, testing and summary all rolled into one if we have time constraints placed on us.

Further reading

Baird, L., Schneier, C. & Laird, D., *The Training and Development Source-book*, Human Resource Press, Massachusetts, 1985, Part 1, Section VII (D).

Craig, Robert, *Training and Development Handbook*, 2nd edn, McGraw-Hill Book Company, New York, 1976, Chapter 10.

Dowling, J. R., Drolet, R. P., *Developing and Administering an Industrial Training Program*, CBI Publishing, Massachusetts, 1979, Part III.

Laird, Dugan, *Approaches to Training and Development*, Addison-Wesley Publishing Company, Massachusetts, 1978, Chapter II.

Mager, Robert, *Measuring Instructional Results*, 2nd edn, Pitman Learning Company, California, 1984.

CHAPTER 15

Difficult situations and nerves

Now let's have a look at the handling of difficult situations and difficult participants. We will also look at a few methods that help to overcome that sweaty-palm syndrome. As well as tips for the new trainer, you will find included in this chapter some suggestions that may be relevant to experienced trainers who need to brush up a bit.

> You must learn to pause now and then
> so that things may catch up to you.

Dealing with difficult situations

All trainers get difficult participants or situations in their sessions. And it happens more often than we would like it to happen.

However difficult a situation seems to be, trainers need to keep their cool

What are some of the situations, and how can we handle them as training professionals?

The group remains silent. It may help to ask the trainees why they are bombarding you with their silence; it may be that they have a good reason. Perhaps you are covering material they have already been presented with. Perhaps they don't understand what's being presented, or perhaps your presentation method needs to be revised.

Things are moving too fast. Sometimes the group will become enthusiastic very quickly. This is good as long as you are prepared for it. You can ask for greater clarification of responses, ask for other participants to comment on responses or simply pose more difficult questions to the individuals or the group.

Things are moving too slowly. It's possible that the group isn't motivated to listen to your presentation. There are other reasons as well, but the same solutions apply. Ask for participant comments by nominating people to reply. Deliberately misstating information can spark comments from the group but if it doesn't it's time to wake them up. You must give them a reason to listen and to become involved. Try to build on things they already know. Don't speed your presentation up to get them moving, it won't work.

A talkative participant. This is quite acceptable as long as the situation doesn't get out of hand. One or two talkative participants can add to the total value of the session. It's only if they become distracting to the rest of the group that you need to step in. Before you step in, try to use their peers to quieten them down. If that fails you can cut the speaker off and summarise what they have said and then move straight on. If nothing else works, talk to them during a break, thank them for their input, but ask them to slow down a bit so that others may participate.

A silent participant. It may be that this person came along just to listen to the presentation. If you need them to participate, you might have to ask them some direct questions. Tread cautiously to start with by asking questions that can be answered fairly easily. If it happens to be a long-serving employee, it may be more relevant to ask them to share their experiences with the group.

The typical know-all. This person will know everything and will correct, confront and contradict you. In most situations the group will sort this problem out for you. It's sometimes useful to get this person to take the notes. Another method is to put the know-all in your blind spot so that you may call on others more easily. This is called politely ignoring them. Don't get them offside, their peers may feel for them.

Sessions getting sidetracked. Sometimes a discussion starts in the right direction but finishes up in the wrong place. The trainer must get it back on line. Perhaps ask the group if this is relevant to the topic, or simply say that, as interesting as it is, we only have enough time to cover the real issues. Make sure the group knows where they are heading to start with, so that they can see when the discussion gets sidetracked.

Personality problems (between participants). Personality problems can distract everyone. If arguments start between participants you must cut in quickly. Ask others for comments on the issue. Try to keep the personalities separated. If necessary speak to them during a break, and if the problem continues you may have to ask them (during a break) to keep their comments to themselves, or ask both of them to leave.

Personality problems (trainer and participant). Occasionally you will find that you have a personality clash with one of your participants. The professional trainer must ignore this and continue treating that participant in a normal manner. Avoid letting the group see the problem.

The rambler. Some participants just ramble on, and on, and on. When they pause it's possible to ask them which point their comments are referring to, particularly if they have an outline of the session. You may have to politely cut them off by thanking them and moving straight on to the next issue. Interrupt politely and summarise before they finish, and cover all of the points you were after.

The arguer. The participant who argues might also have to be placed in a blind spot. Most of the time the group will ask the arguer to quieten down so the session can move on. Use your breaks again to talk to the person, tell them that others are being disadvantaged by their continuous objections. As a final step you may ask them to leave the group.

Complaints about other issues. Make sure that the trainees know this session won't be able to solve the world's problems. If you get complaints about the organisation, let them know that they can't change policy. If you spend time exploring such complaints you'll be wasting the group's time on issues that can't be altered by them or you.

The side conversation. If you find that people become involved in side conversations, ask them to speak up so that the group can hear their comments on the issue. You'll find that this polite, non-threatening intervention will stop them from continuing.

The definitely wrong response. Don't embarrass any participant by telling them that they are wrong. What you can do is to acknowledge that they are entitled to their point of view and that is one way of looking at the situation. You can also summarise their response, using the correct information. Another way is to ask the rest of the group for their comments on that particular response.

Planning the presentation

Planning and organisation are probably the most important points of your presentation. When they are under control everything may just fall into place for you.

Planning includes all of your preparation, and the organisation includes the information to be presented (this ties up with your objectives), who it's to be presented to, how it's to be presented and in what order. It is rather like the planning and organisation of a three-course meal.

The planning is the selection of the menu, deciding who to invite and the cooking of the meal. The presentation is the way the final meal looks, and whether the guests want to eat it or not. This careful preparation assists in the avoidance of difficult situations and tends to settle the nerves as well. All that remains is to stop your hand from shaking as you serve the meal.

How to deal with anxiety

Anxiety or stress is a natural state that exists with trainers when they have to stand in front of a group. New trainers take note, it doesn't disappear. What we manage to do with experience is to turn it to our advantage.

It is unlikely that there is a competent trainer who can stand in front of a group and still have a normal breathing rate, a dry shirt or blouse, a steady hand and a normal pulse rate.

Some of the problems new trainers face with their first lesson are:

- the mouth going dry
- feeling like a stranger in 'strangerland'
- social barriers (age, sex, etc.)
- the subject matter.

Let's look at a number of methods in use that deal with new trainers' nerves and butterflies. By following these tips you may be able to overcome your own nervousness:

- Be at ease and relax. Remember that the participants came to listen to you. They are not likely to begin by being negative.
- Breathe deeply as you walk down the corridor to the group. When people feel nervous their breathing is generally too shallow.
- As you walk down the corridor mentally rehearse the sequence of your presentation.
- Remember the self-fulfilling prophecy. If you think of yourself giving an excellent presentation, you probably will. If you think of yourself making a fool of yourself, again you probably will.
- Again, use the self-fulfilling prophecy and think of yourself as relaxed.
- Arrive early so you can settle in.
- Look professional. Dress the part, and if you have course material with you make sure they can see that you have done your prework. No need to hide it.
- Try to anticipate student questions. Having anticipated the questions, work out the correct responses.
- Check all your support equipment before the presentation so that you know everything is in working order.
- Create a physical setting that you feel comfortable with. If necessary it can be changed later.
- Use your session notes. You spent quite a bit of time preparing them, so use them effectively.
- Make sure that you establish your credibility during the beginning of the session.
- Using your session notes, give the group an outline of the presentation. Let them know what is to happen and what is expected.
- Motivate the group to listen to what you have to say. Give them a need to know.
- Brain-teasers make an interesting introduction if they can be made relevant to the presentation. They take the spotlight off you while you settle down.

- Practise your presentation beforehand. You may feel a little silly doing it to the bathroom mirror, but practice does make perfect. It's generally worthwhile to practise the beginning of your presentation a bit more than the rest. If you are serious about improvement you may even use a video or tape recorder. (Don't use the video in the bathroom as the lens tends to fog up.)
- Recognise that the tension you feel may be used effectively in your presentation. You may even plan this use in your notes, or try it in your practice session in the bathroom. Jump, throw your arms around, or maybe take the lead in a role play.
- Move around. Don't just stand fixed to one spot in front of the group. Walk around, but not so much that you then become a distraction.
- Warm up your voice before you start the presentation. Talk or sing to yourself. If that seems too silly, talk to the participants before the presentation starts.
- Keep eye contact with everyone in the group, don't single out just one or two people.
- You need to be comfortable. Your notes should be in order and placed where you need them to be.
- If you're using a microphone, you must try it well in advance to get used to it. Make sure that it's properly adjusted for your use.
- Pronounce your words clearly. Your audience needs to understand them all.
- Make sure that you know what you're talking about. If you don't, find out quickly or get someone else to do it. Trainers don't need to be experts in the subject matter, but they do have to have more than a good knowledge of the subject.
- If you have to sit in front of the group before your presentation, try some simple unobtrusive isometric exercises. Tense your muscles for a few seconds and then relax them, starting at the feet and working up to the head. Remember that these are unobtrusive exercises, so no one will know that you are doing them.
- Attend appropriate courses in presentation techniques or public speaking.
- Remember that the average adult attention span is, at most, only around twenty minutes. Allow for breaks; they will help you as well.
- Use the nine principles of learning, but in particular use group participation for settling nerves.
- Find out in advance who the participants are and what backgrounds they have.

- Admit your mistakes, but only if you make them. It may be of benefit to make the occasional mistake, this will let them see you as one of them. The mistake may also be used to check their understanding.
- You must always appear to be enthusiastic, even when you're not. With practice, anxiety can be changed to enthusiasm.
- Set up a video or tape recorder to see how you feel as a participant watching or listening to your session.
- Develop your own style of presentation. Don't always try to copy others.
- Get feedback from the participants. What you think you're saying may not be what they are hearing.
- Don't read from the text, the participants can read the material in their own time. This also allows you to use your own words, which are generally easier for the group to understand.
- Don't have heavy nights before a day of presentations. You need to be well-rested and on your toes.

Conclusion

Feeling dry in the mouth and having a few nervous twitches are normal for all trainers, both new and experienced. If you don't feel at least a little bit anxious it may be time to look for a new challenge in your career.

Put your mind into gear before opening your mouth. This is good advice for anyone, but is particularly important for someone standing in front of a group.

It's important for trainers to be polite to everyone in the group. If we aren't, we may find that the group turns on us if we pick on someone, even if that person is someone the whole group appears not to tolerate.

If you have a difficult participant try to use the peer pressure in the group to sort the problem out for you. Peer pressure is an excellent way of overcoming such problems, so use it to your advantage.

Don't single people out in a group situation; instead, talk to them during breaks. You may have to call extra breaks occasionally.

A number of methods useful for calming nerves have been included in this chapter. Use them, all of them, if possible. Not only will it be easier for you to present your session, it will make it easier for your participants to absorb the information.

Application example

Before becoming a trainer you probably attended a number of presentations given by other people. It is likely that you witnessed a number of difficult situations. Think back on those presentations and see if you can recall how they were handled by the presenter. The next time you sit in the audience of a presentation watch specifically for these situations and see if the methods used to handle them will suit your style.

Further reading

Donaldson, Les & Scannell, Edward, *Human Resource Development*, 2nd edn, Addison-Wesley Publishing Company, Massachusetts, 1986, Chapters 16 and 18.

CHAPTER 16

Motivation and attention

Why do you continue to do certain things and not others? Why do you listen only to some people?

It's all to do with motivation and the way our attention is held. If we want our participants to learn, we must motivate them to listen to us and ensure that we keep their attention. When we make a presentation who do you think is responsible for the individual's learning? The trainer is.

What is motivation?

Motivation is the urge in the individual to have a need filled. The need or urge becomes more powerful when it's not being satisfied.

The more motivated the participants are, the easier it is for the trainer to train effectively. If the participants are not motivated to listen or learn they are almost certainly wasting their time and yours.

Believe it or not, the trainer is responsible in most cases for motivating the participants. It doesn't happen automatically. But before we look at some motivation techniques, we need to recognise that there are two types of motivation. The first type is where participants know that they must perform in the course or they may suffer severe consequences. This is referred to as a negative motivator. The second and more effective form of motivation is when the participants simply want to learn. This form of motivation creates a more pleasant learning atmosphere.

We will be dealing only with the second form of motivation as it's the one normally used. The threatening form of motivation is used in extreme situations where other methods may not work or have already failed.

How do we motivate a participant?

If we believe that motivation is the urge in the individual to have a need filled, wouldn't it be logical to say that if we could identify what need the participants have, we could motivate or interest them to listen? This is almost right, but it needs some refining.

If we've done our job properly the group will respond to the information that the course or presentation is based on. This information should tie in with their needs which should have been correctly identified in the needs analysis.

At the beginning of the first few sessions the trainer can allow the group to contribute ideas about the direction of the course and the selection of specific topic areas. This type of course is commonly referred to as user-driven. If the group has this input it then becomes their own design. With this design comes a sense of ownership which is a great motivator. If they think that they have chosen the topic areas they can't complain during the course that you have given them irrelevant information.

You will probably find that the areas identified by the group in this situation match up with your course objectives. If they do not match up exactly you may have to give them a bit of subtle direction.

You have to let the individuals know that by listening or participating in your session they will have some of their needs filled. It's up to you to identify these needs and describe them. These needs can come from many different areas: social needs, safety needs, security needs, status, new technology, promotion opportunities, new machinery, new methods, or simply an easier way to do the job.

Motivating the participants is similar to dangling the proverbial carrot in front of them, but they always get the carrot when they finish.

Regardless of what your session is about, you can always find some reason for encouraging the participants to listen. Once the reason has been stated it creates the motivation.

There are a number of motivation theories that are interesting to read and study. However, the easiest and most practical thing new trainers can do is to ask themselves 'If I were a participant on this course, why should I listen to me?'

If you pose this question you will always find some motivating response, even if it takes several minutes. But don't stop at one. The more reasons you can give for someone to listen to your presentation the more they will be motivated. Remember, too, it's the trainer's responsibility to remind the participants that they want to learn and to supply them with the incentive.

It may also help if you keep one or two of your motivators up your sleeve in case things start to drag and you need to fire their motivation or grab attention again during the session.

Even if you're involved in a presentation which hasn't been designed for a stated need through a training needs analysis, you can talk to the group before the session starts to identify their needs. If this can't be done, you should plan a few minutes at the beginning of the session to find their needs and link the session to those needs.

If you think it sounds as though you're becoming a salesperson, you're right. You must sell your reasons for motivation to all of the individuals in the group.

Using the nine principles of learning properly will help to create motivation and will also allow you to keep the group's interest during the session. Make sure that you use them effectively.

If the trainees realise that their needs will be met they are usually eager to learn

Conclusion

It's important that we motivate the individuals in the group to want to listen, learn or participate. Without motivation they won't do anything. Once we have created motivation we sometimes still need to remind the group of their reasons for wanting to learn. By using these reminders, and the nine principles of adult learning, we can keep the group's attention.

We must know our audience in advance so that we can identify their motivators. Sometimes we only find out about our audience thirty minutes before the session commences. A good trainer is flexible and will adapt to suit the specific group needs as they appear.

> PEOPLE DO THINGS FOR THEIR REASONS,
> NOT YOURS
> OR THE ORGANIZATION'S.

You may need to recapture the trainees' attention during a session, so keep some tactics in reserve

Application example

The day is hot, the winds are calm and it feels like a holiday atmosphere. Can you imagine sitting in an open classroom next to a white sandy beach, overlooking the warm waters, on a tropical island? That's what your participants see, but you've been given a four-hour session to present on law. Some solutions have to be found for this interesting problem.

For this presentation the trainer had to find out very quickly (only a couple of days before the session started) what the needs of the group were. The trainer found that the participants were very concerned about implications of both omission and commission. This piece of information was what the trainer needed for the group's motivation and attention.

The session started with the trainer nominating participants to act in various roles, judge, jury, defendant, recorders and other court personnel.

Sometimes a dramatic illustration can be invaluable in getting the group's attention

Before any questions were asked the trainer explained that one of the participants had been charged in the areas of omission and commission during the supervision of the plaintiff's daughter. Their task was to listen to the evidence and pass judgment (and possibly sentence) on the defendant.

Everybody was motivated to listen and participate, as the trainer had found an excellent reason for them to listen. This need was found by simply talking to them.

The next thing to happen after the ground rules had been set was for a number of pallbearers to carry in a coffin containing, supposedly, the blood-covered body of the plaintiff's daughter. The coffin was placed in the centre of the 'classroom'.

Do you think the trainer had the group's attention? It could have been snowing green snow and the group wouldn't have noticed!

Further reading

Baird, L., Schneier, C. & Laird, D., *The Training and Development Sourcebook*, Human Resource Press, Massachusetts, 1985, Part 1, Section VII (A).

Donaldson, Les & Scannell, Edward, *Human Resource Development: The New Trainer's Guide*, 2nd edn, Addison-Wesley Publishing Company, Massachusetts, 1986, Chapter II.

Owens, Robert, *Organisational Behaviour in Education*, 3rd edn, Prentice Hall International, New Jersey, 1987, Chapter 4.

CHAPTER 17

Barriers to effective communication

All trainers must recognise that there are many barriers to effective communication with both individuals and with groups of people.

In this chapter I will attempt to give you most of the common barriers to effective communication so that you may be able to recognise them should you experience any of them. Not only should you recognise them, you must be able to fix them.

What is effective communication?

Before starting, it will help if we define what communication is. Unfortunately there are still some people who think communication is simply being able to give clear directions or information. This understanding of communication is only half right.

Communication is the effective giving and receiving of information. To be effective, the message must be understood by both the communicator and the receiver. If the message isn't clearly or easily understood there is a problem that needs to be rectified. Such problems are our barriers to effective communication.

In most communication models we have a message (the instruction) that needs to be given to another person. When the message sender (the trainer) selects who to give the message to (the participant), they need to select an appropriate medium for the sending of the message. The message is then sent, in the appropriate form, and received. The message receiver interprets the message and perhaps adds their own meaning to some or all of it. As this is a fairly complicated exercise there is always the chance of things going wrong.

The only way to find out if the message has been received and understood without any distortion is to get feedback from the message receiver.

This process of message sending and receiving may involve the spoken word, nonverbal gestures, written information or any other means that you can think of.

You must realise that regardless of which process you're using, all are susceptible to distortion or misunderstanding.

Communication does not occur unless there is a clear understanding by both parties

What are the common barriers?

The use of long words by the trainer is quite often a problem. Have you been in a presentation where the trainer has tried to impress the participants with long words? You normally find that nobody is prepared to ask what they all mean as they have a fear of looking ignorant in front of the group. Use only easily understood language.

Using new words is quite valid as long as you realise that they are new to the group and that you explain their meaning.

Jargon should be avoided unless it's relevant to the training or to the group's general knowledge. If it is used its meaning must be explained. Jargon can be difficult to identify as we often use it without even noticing. We also have the situation where your participants might not ask what it means for fear of looking ignorant.

Language differences are becoming more of a problem as we have an increasing percentage of different language groups at our venues. Make sure that you speak clearly and keep testing for message understanding.

Feedback helps us to find out if our message has been properly understood

When the nonverbal message does not match the verbal message there is a barrier. We can't afford to create confusion by having our nonverbal communication saying something different to our verbal communication.

If training aids don't match the topic we again create confusion. When we select our training aids we must make certain that they are appropriate to the topic.

If the training aids don't work when they're supposed to, the participant may lose interest. Check before starting that all of your training aids work, particularly models and samples you have ready for the group to use.

A boring presentation can be one of your biggest barriers to effective communication. If you have a boring topic you must find a way to liven it up. If you're simply a boring presenter, design the session in such a way that your own presentation does not take too long.

Assuming they know all of the things that should be prerequisite to them attending your presentation. You need to check existing levels of knowledge at the very beginning of your presentation. Make sure that your session builds on existing participant knowledge.

The way we say things can affect the meaning and therefore the understanding. Most trainers, without realising it, tend to speak louder when they're talking about important sections of their presentation. Try to change this around, the participants might pay more attention to the minor points of the presentation. Think about your projection and inflections.

Participant and trainer preconceptions have to match up. Any preconceived ideas the participants have about the presentation must be accurate. Make certain that the participants know what the presentation is about before it starts. It's also a good idea to send out course information to the participants well before the course commences.

By listening to the individuals and the group you'll find out if your message is getting through clearly and safely. Remember that communication is a two-way process and that you continually have to get feedback from the group to check understanding.

Make sure that the trainees know in advance what the training session will be about

Why do some participants not listen?

In addition to the previous list of barriers we also need to recognise some other reasons why the participants may not be listening to your presentation. If your participants are not listening you could safely say that communication has broken down.

Remember that people think faster than your speaking rate, so pace your presentation to stop their minds from wandering. Most trainers find it best if the pace varies during the session.

Effective listening requires you to give the group members some motivation. If they do not know why they should listen to your presentation, they probably will not listen.

Distractions also interfere with listening. When the participants are distracted by your upside down overhead transparency, or by the handout that you've given out too early, they concentrate on the distraction and not on your presentation.

If the information becomes too complicated, effective listening stops. If you have complex information to pass on, make a point of breaking the information down into small, easily understandable pieces. Check the

> ONE SHOULD NOT AIM AT BEING
> POSSIBLE TO UNDERSTAND,
> ONE SHOULD AIM AT BEING
> IMPOSSIBLE TO MISUNDERSTAND.

Poor communication may result in:

- Poor training of staff
  - Misunderstandings
    - Conflict between staff
      - Objectives not being met
        - Frustration
          - Organisational inefficiency

group's understanding before moving on to the next piece and so avoid information overload.

Alternatively, if the information is too simple, participants will again let their thoughts drift elsewhere. Once the mind starts wandering, effective listening stops. Your presentation must be challenging to the individuals.

Many books and articles have been written on effective listening skills. I suggest that you find an article or two and read them. It's imperative that the trainer is a good listener as well as a good presenter.

Conclusion

We want participants to interpret the information correctly. To receive the message without distortion, individuals must be listening attentively. It also helps if the group respects you as a trainer. You need to gain this respect, it doesn't just come with the job.

Ask yourself, 'is this the best way to get my message across?' It may be that there are more effective ways. Whichever is the easiest way for the participants to understand is the one that should be used. Make certain that you always consider the receiver.

Even simple communication needs to be planned in advance. If you don't understand your message, how is someone else supposed to understand you?

Communication is the effective process of information giving and receiving, but to be effective the message must be understood by both the communicator and the receiver. Always follow up your message.

Application example

As a new trainer it's sometimes interesting to talk with your group informally after the presentation. You may find that things you thought were perfectly clear have been interpreted in a completely different way.

Make mental notes of the reasons for the misunderstanding. Don't try to defend your communication; if the correct message didn't get across, you need to modify the delivery.

When working with other trainers, it's a good idea to offer constructive criticism on the communication. It's sometimes very difficult to identify the barriers by yourself, so help each other improve effective communication skills.

Further reading

Craig, Robert, *Training and Development Handbook*, 2nd edn, McGraw-Hill Book Company, New York, 1976, Chapter 31.

Donaldson, Les & Scannell, Edward, *Human Resource Development: The New Trainer's Guide*, 2nd edn, Addison-Wesley Publishing Company, Massachusetts, 1986, Chapter 9.

Morris, Kenneth & Cinnamon, Kenneth, *A Handbook of Non-verbal Group Exercises*, Applied Skills Press, California, 1983.

Morris, Kenneth & Cinnamon, Kenneth, *A Handbook of Verbal Group Exercises*, Applied Skills Press, California, 1983.

CHAPTER 18

Nonverbal communication

If you want your participants to be enthusiastic about your presentation you need to communicate your enthusiasm to them. A trainer standing, nervously, in front of a group and holding on to the lectern for dear life isn't going to project enthusiasm. Even before the trainer has said anything the group knows what to expect. On the other hand a trainer who is dressed appropriately and looks relaxed and enthusiastic will have much more chance of reaching the session objectives.

Recent studies indicate that around 65 per cent of our communication is done through nonverbal signals. Trainers should be experts in communication, so it follows that they must know about these signals. Nonverbal communication is also referred to as body language and it is a study in itself. However, to assist the new trainer we will attempt to identify a number of the most common nonverbal communications the trainer is likely to encounter.

What is nonverbal communication?

Nonverbal communication is anything that can alter or reinforce the message in any form of communication. If you think that this is a very broad definition, and covers all types of communication, you are right.

Your facial expression is just part of your non-verbal communication

129

We communicate nonverbally by the way we dress, our posture, the expressions on our face, the amount of eye contact used, the way we position our hands, the way we touch things and the way we listen.

Even a simple statement can have its meaning altered or reinforced by the way we shrug our shoulders when we put it to the group, by the use of inflection when we say it, by the way it is written or typed when we give it out as a handout. Perhaps the figure of 65 per cent is extremely conservative.

Gestures, dress and posture all add meaning to what we actually say

What gestures should we be aware of?

Some participants require more personal space than others. If they don't have this space they feel uncomfortable and therefore do not pay attention to the presentation. Watch for signs.

If you ask a participant whether they understand what you're talking about and they say 'yes', make sure that the head gesture (nodding) matches, and isn't in conflict with, the stated response.

When a question is being asked of you, you should watch the person asking it. It is sometimes easy to pick up clues as to what they *really* want to know.

If a participant covers their mouth while you are speaking it may indicate that they don't believe you. It may be worthwhile checking this before you go further.

If your participants use both their hands to support their heads it's time to change your tactics, boredom has set in.

When the head is supported by one hand and that hand has a finger pointing vertically, it suggests that the person is evaluating the information you've just given.

If someone in the group starts pulling at their collar, it may indicate that they are getting angry and need to let off some steam.

Should your participants start rubbing their hands together, watch out, you may be being conned.

Palm gestures are not often used in training rooms as the participants are usually seated. However, if someone presents you with open palms it's safe to assume that they are being totally honest with you.

A church steeple formed by the hands is used by the person who knows everything about the subject. Find out if they do have the knowledge. If they have, encourage them to participate and offer their ideas. Look for their support.

Similarly the person who thinks they know everything may adopt a sitting back position with the hands clasped behind the head. Check their understanding and knowledge and try to enlist their support.

Folded arms can indicate that the participant has put up a barrier. However when people sit for long periods of time they tend to fold their arms more often.

How can we detect uncertainty?

If we ask a participant a question and, while they are responding, they attempt to cover their mouth, it may indicate that they are trying to hide what they are saying.

Similarly if a person rubs their nose while answering or talking it may again indicate that they are uncertain, or lying about their response.

Looking down and rubbing an eye can also indicate a lie or uncertainty. It may indicate that they can't see, or don't want to see, the point you are making.

These points are only indicators and should not be taken as gospel. These gestures merely give you an indication that the person may not be telling the truth, or that they don't believe what you are saying.

Are all people the same?

Each sex, social class, age, nationality, race or culture has its own set of built-in nonverbal signals. When a person is educated in that society not only are they taught the words or spoken language, they also learn the nonverbal signals of that society.

For this reason we can't say that because a person uses a specific gesture they are communicating a known message. In some societies if eye contact is avoided it can indicate that a person may be hiding the truth when asked a question. In other societies this same gesture may indicate respect for the person asking the question.

We need to be aware of our own preconceived ideas. You may think it's easy to classify some participants on one or two nonverbal actions, but question yourself on the interpretation you've made. Nonverbal signals sometimes need to be clarified as we do with verbal signals when we are uncertain of the meaning.

Conclusion

It's easy to see that we do rely heavily on the nonverbal gestures given by others. If we ignore them we may not get the whole picture. If we do take them in, it may lead us to what the participant is really thinking. At the very least it reinforces what they are saying.

One signal or gesture by itself probably won't indicate anything at all. What we should be doing is looking for groups of signals. If we notice two gestures that have similar interpretations, we should take action on them, at least by checking the participant's message.

Not only do these gestures apply to the participants, they also apply to you as the trainer. When you say something to the group you have to ensure that your nonverbal signals match your message. Don't say yes to someone in the group while shaking your head from side to side, or when you tell the group that you are open to questions make sure that your arms aren't folded tightly across your chest.

Remember that nonverbal communication is important in both the delivering and receiving of a message. Don't try to hide your own nonverbal signals.

Application example

Most of the time we are unaware of our own nonverbal signals. In the last chapter I suggested that if you use another trainer to check your effective communication with a group, they would be able to offer constructive criticism. This would also apply to your non-verbal communication with the group.

If this is impractical or impossible, why not set up a video camera in the back of your classroom? Then you will be able to see all of the things you wouldn't have believed you were doing.

Once you start to understand nonverbal signals, you will find that not only do you look for them in a training situation, you will look for them outside the classroom as well. It may even become part of your normal communication process.

Further reading

Morris, Kenneth & Cinnamon, Kenneth, *A Handbook of Nonverbal Group Exercises*, Applied Skills Press, California, 1983.

Pease, Allan, *Body Language*, Camel Publishing Company, North Sydney, 1981.

CHAPTER 19

Testing

Tests and their purpose

A test is some form of training measurement device that trainers can use to determine whether learning has taken, or is taking place. The term 'test' is now very complicated. I will be looking at the simpler interpretations rather than trying to explain the psychological meanings.

The purpose of testing is to give us an indication of trainee knowledge, understanding or behaviour. We can use a test to identify competencies and so establish entry levels of students before they attend training. This is useful because it saves us training in subjects the trainees already understand well.

Alternatively, it may reveal gaps we had not suspected were there. Either way, it gives us a starting point for the course, allowing us to build or link to things that the trainee has identified as knowing. These tests are called pre-course tests.

A test can be, and is, used during the course of instruction to check student knowledge, understanding or change in behaviour. If the trainee is understanding what the session is about and how it all works, we can give them positive feedback through the tests. This is a good trainee motivator and generally a trainer motivator as well. If, however, we find that the test results aren't as good as we had required, we may need to do some quick revision. It would be pointless to continue when only the trainer understands what was happening, and why.

Poor test results could indicate that the majority of the group doesn't understand your method of instruction, or they don't understand the material being presented, or the test isn't relevant, or any number of things. If you do get poor test results from the majority of the group, you must examine the results to find out why. This examination must be carried out quickly as you are probably running out of course time.

Don't let your students dwell on poor test results. If they start thinking that they're going to fail your course, they might do so. Remember the self-fulfilling prophecy?

The predominant purpose of tests is for student and instructor feedback. We have already discussed the importance to the students, but the instructor usually uses test results to modify and improve the training. If the test results are poor the instructor looks at the students first. If they do not seem to provide an answer, the trainers must look at their own work for the answer. Perhaps there was something wrong with the material or with the instruction. Maybe it's a combination of both. The trainer must fix this problem which has been shown through testing.

The test material should be designed when we write our session or course objectives. It must be a test to see if the trainees have reached the stated objectives and we must decide on the criteria for passing or failing.

When we design our tests we must also consider how the trainees are to pass or fail; a true test should be a test of the stated objectives.

If we are testing the objectives the trainee more than likely can or cannot meet the criteria set. If this is the case maybe they pass if they can 'do it' within set criteria; otherwise they fail.

Many trainers still use a graded system of marking which has its advantages in a few situations, but not many. It's often hard to explain that two trainees can perform the same task to the same standard, but one got an 'A' while the other a 'B'. If they both performed the task, shouldn't they both simply pass?

Perhaps we should examine our marking system when we design our test.

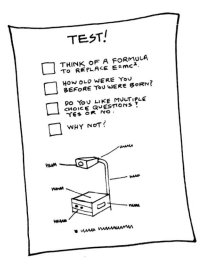

Tests are useful for both the students and trainers to measure their own performance

When should we test?

We've already mentioned that we can test participants before they attend training. When we conducted the training needs analysis for a course we probably used some form of testing then. If so, why not use it?

We should also test our participants during the course of instruction. It would be ridiculous to get to the end of a three-month training course and then find that the participants had not achieved the first few session objectives.

It's a good idea to test often during the course of instruction. Use a methodical system so you don't forget. If you're instructing in something that is critical for the students to understand, test more frequently.

Testing should also be carried out at the end of formal training. As the students finish in the classroom, give them an end-of-course test to find out if they have met the course objectives. Most students expect this test and sometimes feel cheated if they don't get a chance to show how much they have learnt. Their supervisors are generally interested in these results too. End-of-course testing also helps the trainer to compile course information.

The final type of test that we carry out is when the participant is back on-the-job. When the participant left the classroom, we knew that they could use the instruction we had given them. If we follow the participant on-the-job we can find out if they are applying the instruction we gave them and if the instruction is having the desired result. This shows whether or not the training gap, originally identified in our training needs analysis, has been filled.

Regardless of the type of test, we need to pilot our test to see if it's fully understood and to find out if it needs any modification.

Types of tests

There are many types of tests but we will be dealing only with the more common types in this chapter. The choice of type is up to you, but remember that you are trying to find out if they know what they should know right now, not in future sessions.

We aren't trying to show them how smart we are, either. Design the test so that everyone can understand what is being asked.

Essays. If requesting an essay answer the trainer must state, in the question, exactly what is required of the student. It should give the student a lead-in to the answer.

Sample: In 300–500 words describe the nine principles of learning. You are required to give examples of each of these principles.

A marking guide must also be designed. It should list all the points that you expect the trainee to cover, and it will also tell you how the marks are to be awarded. A marking guide is essential for others who may be helping you with the marking, or if students question their results. If a student got a mark of 70 per cent you should be able to let them know which 30 per cent they missed out on.

Oral testing. This form of testing is used more often than most people realise. When you're in any training situation the session leaders are usually asking questions of the group. These questions are an informal type of oral test.

Oral tests can require either oral or written responses. If you require written responses make sure that you allow enough time for the students to write their answers.

It's important that you speak clearly when you deliver your question. If the message isn't received properly there isn't much point in going on.

Multiple choice. This is an excellent way of testing if the test has been designed properly. It's usually quick and accurate in testing knowledge.

When designing a multiple-choice test, consider the following:

- make the layout easy for yourself to mark
- have all of the question in the first part, don't repeat it in all of the responses
- the questions must be relevant to the subject
- don't try to trick people
- avoid double negatives

    Example: Which of the following isn't true of trainers?
    A. trainers cannot survive without classrooms
    B. trainers cannot survive without resources
    C. trainers don't survive without trainees
    D. trainers don't survive without objectives
    (See how confusing double negatives are?)

- scatter the responses evenly over the selection of choices (about 25 per cent each for A, B, C and D)
- consider the amount the student would be able to guess (25 per cent right if only four responses to choose from)
- pictures or diagrams may make the test more meaningful

Example: The figure below shows an overhead projector. Which statement is false?

A points to the focusing knob
B points to the on/off switch
C points to the lens head
D points to the purge button

- don't have more than one answer which may be the correct response
- don't use textbook answers all the time (they can be recognised as being right).

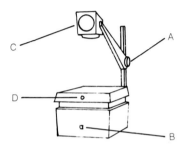

Diagrams and multiple choice questions can be useful if you are designing a quick test of knowledge

True and false. True and false tests are handy for the testing of facts. They're quick and easy to mark. However only having the two responses can distort the results as it's possible to get a 50 per cent mark by only guessing the answers.

Consider the following when designing true and false tests:

- the example must be 100 per cent true or 100 per cent false
- avoid double negatives
- about half of your answers should be true and half false
- questions or statements to be kept short. (The following shows how they may become confusing if too long.)

Example: Evaluation is the opinion or judgment we make from the data that has been collected. If the end measurement is counted or valued with the same system we used during the training needs analysis, we should then be able to see (evaluate) whether the training has been effective.

True ☐

False ☐

- questions or statements must be easy to understand
- design the test so that the response can be circled or ticked
- avoid words like always, never, frequently, rarely, sometimes, occasionally, etc. (they tend to indicate the correct response)
- avoid using textbook quotes.

Performance testing. The performance test can be used when the student should be able to do something. It's important that some form of marking system be devised and strictly adhered to. This allows the trainer to explain a student's mark if necessary. Also, you will need to set time limits for the performance in most cases. Remember that the test is a test to see if the objectives are being met, and both the trainer and the trainee should know what the objectives are.

Refer back to Chapter 7 for more information on performance testing.

Short answer. Short-answer tests are similar to essays but they have different advantages. The test can cover more areas than is possible with an essay and there is less chance of the student misinterpreting the question.

With short-answer questions you will still need to design a marking guide for you or others to use. The questions must be understood by the trainee and should include exact instructions.

Observation. Observation isn't at present a formal type of test. It's generally used well after the end of training to see if the trainees are applying their new knowledge. It has the advantage of testing them without applying examination-type pressures.

For more information on observation go back to Chapter 12.

Test tips for your students

It's up to the individual trainer to determine whether they're going to pass on tips about tests in advance. Some trainers don't believe in giving this information, while others design such a session into the course.

There are lots of things you can tell your students that may help them with examinations. You probably have a few of your own techniques that work for you. Listed below are a few points which may be of assistance.

Some tips for you to give to students:

- read through notes taken during sessions
- read through handout material
- form study groups with other class members

- ask for advice from the educators
- it's important to study often
- try to guess what the questions may be about (remember the objectives)
- look for previous test papers
- don't try to cram just before tests
- keep your cool during the examination
- read the whole test paper before you start
- plan your timing for each question or section
- check your answers when you finish your paper (there's generally sufficient time left).

Conclusion

There are many different types of tests and the trainer needs to select the type of test that's appropriate for the material. If you have a course on typing don't give a handwritten essay test, give a practical typing test. Common sense, isn't it?

When you design your tests try to use variety. Make tests easy to understand; state exactly what you want; test the stated objectives; have the tests checked before you use them; and make sure that you know the correct required answers. A test isn't a battle of wits between the trainer and the trainee. Gone are the days of the trainer trying to design a test that only a few students will pass.

Ensure that the students get the results of their tests as soon as possible. Immediate feedback would be best of all.

Application example

You've been given a group of people to train as trainers and when you make enquiries you find that a training needs analysis has been carried out in the organisation. You have been able to get a copy of the analysis, but it has some deficiencies in it; it hasn't fully determined what these people need to know.

What you must do now is to design a questionnaire to help determine the entry level of the nominated participants. When these pre-course questionnaires are completed it will enable you to determine the course content and to write the session objectives.

As you're writing the session objectives you should also write the end-of-session or end-of-course tests. Include in your plan any important questions to be asked of the participants during the session.

If you write the end-of-session tests with the objectives, you can be reasonably certain that you will be testing the objectives and not something else. Even at this planning stage you should still check to make sure that they match.

After the course is over, to be truly effective, you should go out into the field to correct more information. This can also be done in the form of a questionnaire. It should test the participants to find out what they remember of the new skills or knowledge they learnt in the classroom and to see if they're applying them on the job.

Even if a test does not involve a pass or fail assessment you must still give the participants the results of the test, questionnaire or survey. By giving the results you're letting them know that the information is being used.

When all of these tests have been done, you can write up the results and pass the results or evaluation on to management. Your careful planning should give you confidence in the evaluation results.

Further reading

Craig, Robert, *Training and Development Handbook*, 2nd edn, McGraw-Hill Book Company, New York, 1976, Chapter 10.

Dowling, J. R. & Drolel, R. P., *Developing and Administering an Industrial Training Program*, CBI Publishing, Massachusetts, 1979, Part III.

Field, Laurie, *Teaching Practical Work at TAFE*, Published by ITATE, Sydney, 1984.

Mager, Robert, *Measuring Instructional Results*, 2nd edn, Pitman Learning Company, California, 1984.

CHAPTER 20

Training aids

We learn   1% through taste
           1.5% through touch
           3.5% through smell
           11% through hearing
           83% through sight
We remember 10% of what we read
           20% of what we hear
           30% of what we see
           50% of what we see and hear
           80% of what we say
           90% of what we say and do.

Rigg

What are training aids?

Training aids are strictly aids to learning. They are not a crutch for the instructor to lean on, or something that must be used all the time.

Training aids are things that the trainer can use, with or without words, which facilitate the students' learning. Visual aids are things that the trainees can see. Research has indicated that average trainees will remember only about 20 per cent of what they hear and that they remember between 50 per cent and 80 per cent of what they both hear and see. When we listen, our mind appears to be very selective about what it remembers. It seems to pick up only the things that it's interested in and ignores the rest of the information.

However, if we combine some form of visual aid with the talking, it seems to reinforce key words in the mind. We must take advantage of these aids as this can increase the students' power of recall by 250 to 400 per cent.

If training aids are presented in a simple and logical manner, it not only makes the session easier for the student but easier for the trainer. Another thing that makes it easier for the trainer is that it ensures some consistency in repeat presentations. Training aids also allow other trainers to assist as they too can 'read' what has to be covered. (Obviously they would combine the session notes with the training aids to get the whole picture.)

Training aids can also create interest in the subject. If the aids are presented properly they should catch the students' attention and get them into the learning atmosphere. What we do need to be aware of though is not to become a presenter of training aids. If people only come along to watch the show they probably won't be learning anything. Be wise and be selective. When you use training aids make sure that all of the participants can see, hear, touch, smell or taste whatever it is you want them to.

Most professional trainers use a variety of training aids to keep the trainees interested.

Not all training aids need to be expensive. As most training aids are visual aids they need to be tidy in appearance and generally attractive. They need to be able to hold the trainees' attention and get key points across.

The purpose of visual aids

They arouse and maintain interest.
They simplify instruction.
They accelerate learning as more senses are involved.
They aid retention if a strong impact was made.

Types of training aids

Overhead projector. The overhead projector is one of the most commonly used training aids. It is an electronically operated machine, with a light source at the base which is reflected up to the projection head. From the projection head, the light is projected on to a screen or wall. Between the light source at the base and the projection head we place a transparency containing the information we want the audience to see. Look at the diagram on the following page.

When using an overhead projector for the first time make sure that you're comfortable with it. This means that you should find an empty training room and practise with one and become proficient.

The overhead projector is a very useful training aid

Things all trainers should check when using an overhead projector:

- is the room too light?
- is the projector in focus?
- is the transparency the right way round?
- is the lettering large enough?
- can everyone see the screen?
- do I need a pointer?
- do I have a sheet of paper for revealing bits at a time?
- where is the spare globe?

If you move the overhead projector during your presentation you will need to re-focus it if you place it in a slightly different position.

Chapter 21 gives much more information on the overhead projector and the production of transparencies.

Videos. Video systems are relatively new in the area of training. When we refer to 'video' we are not talking only about video tapes, we are also referring to the use of video cameras for training purposes.

There are currently four types of video:

- U matic (20 mm wide tape)
- VHS (12 mm wide tape)
- Beta (12 mm wide tape)
- Video 8 (8 mm wide tape).

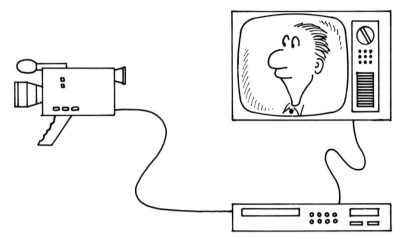

A video camera can be used for on-the-spot filming in the classroom and pre-recorded tapes can be most instructive too

Most of the videos we purchase for training are the same as the 16 mm or 35 mm films we purchase or hire. The advantage of having them on video-tape, though, is that we have a much smaller package to carry around and, more importantly, we can usually use them in a lighted situation. This allows the participants to make notes if they wish to.

Using the video camera is possibly one of the most enlightening experiences trainees can have. When you tell the trainee that they fiddle with their pen too much when they're counselling someone but they don't really believe you, all you now have to do is replay the tape and let them see for themselves.

When using the video camera and player there are a number of things to consider. Listed below are the ones that the new trainer must be aware of.

- preview recorded tapes before the session
- use only one pre-recorded tape for the session
- ensure you have enough power outlets
- make sure all the participants can see the screen
- rewind all tapes when finished
- turn the monitor off when not in use
- keep the lens cap on the camera when not in use
- don't zoom or pan too much with the camera
- try to capture nonverbal signs of the role-players
- allow time for the tapes to be reviewed by the group
- be thoroughly familiar with the equipment
- try to have spares standing by (just in case).

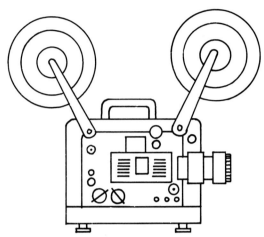

If you intend using a 16 mm film projector be sure that you are practised in its operation

Films. Films used to be very popular with trainers. However, as the result of problems associated with carrying large film containers from class to class and carrying heavy projectors around, we now see them being replaced with videos.

The 16 mm film can be an extremely effective training aid. Normally these films are narrated by a well-known personality or an expert in the field and can have a lot of impact.

Projectors for 16 mm film aren't easy to set up and the trainer or an assistant must enter the training room well before the session to prepare for the screening.

To use a film projector effectively make sure you read the instruction booklet, or get someone to show you how to use it. If you get someone to show you, these are the things that you should be asking:

- where should I set it up?
- how do I load it?
- how do I rewind the film?
- how does it pack up?
- where is the spare globe?
- when can I preview the film?
- can I try it now?

Whiteboards. As new training rooms are being built the chalkboard is gradually being replaced with whiteboards. A whiteboard is a smooth white-surfaced board which can be written on with special whiteboard markers. The white surface is much nicer to look at in contrast to the darker coloured chalkboards.

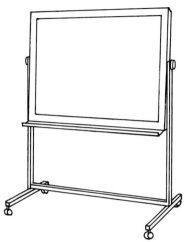

The mobile whiteboard can double as an overhead projector screen

Whiteboards are generally mounted on portable wheeled frames which allows us to have a portable training room. This portability makes it an attractive proposition for the management of most organisations.

As with the use of most training aids there are a number of things to remember when using the whiteboard:

- have the whiteboard positioned so that everyone can see it
- write large enough for everyone to see
- write legibly (if you can't, practise)
- put the cap on the marker when you're not using it (they dry out very quickly)
- use a variety of colours
- use the eraser provided to erase with
- plan your board layout before you start writing
- don't put too much on the board
- never talk to the board. Write, then turn and talk
- practise drawing straight lines, circles and letters on the whiteboard as often as possible
- if you use the whiteboard as a projection screen, make sure that the reflection off the screen is not directed at anyone in the group. (Check the back of the screen, it may have a matt projection finish.)
- don't bang the tip of the whiteboard marker on the board, it pushes the tip back into the casing and makes it useless.

Chalkboards. Chalkboards are still a common sight in training rooms. The principle here is to have a matt painted surface which can be written on

Chalkboards are still popular and can be used very effectively

using a piece of chalk. Gone are the days of having chalk dust everywhere, we can now purchase dustless and squeakless chalk.

There are a few tricks you can use with a chalkboard. Some of them are detailed below.

- plan your layout before you start writing
- don't put too much on the board at once
- always erase with the duster provided
- use coloured chalk to highlight
- make fast, firm strokes with the chalk
- never talk to the board. Write, then turn and talk
- hold the chalk between your thumb and the first two fingers with about 1 to 2 cm of chalk projecting
- rotate the chalk as you write to keep a good writing point
- use templates to assist with the drawing of diagrams
- using a diagram on a large sheet of paper, go along the lines punching pin holes. Hold the paper up on the board and tap it with the duster. When you take the paper away, simply join the dots for a professional-looking diagram. All this is done before the group comes in
- use an overhead projector to project your diagrams up on the chalkboard. Then copy them before the group comes in
- practise drawing straight lines, circles and letters on the chalkboard as often as possible.

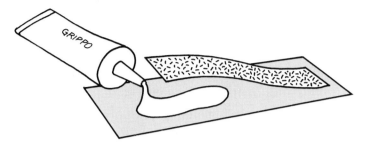

If you prepare training materials well in advance the feltboard is an ideal way to display them

Feltboards. Feltboards or blanket boards may be used for the display of any prepared materials. If you have a series of diagrams that you wish to use, glue some coarse sandpaper on the back of them. The sandpaper will attach to the felt surface.

Magnetic boards. Magnetic boards are usually a painted sheet of steel. The boards themselves are not magnetic, but the things we stick on them are. Again if you have a series of diagrams that you wish to present, it's a matter of sticking magnets on the back of your diagrams. Magnets like the ones we use to hold notes on refrigerator doors are ideal and can now be purchased quite easily. Sometimes you may find that your whiteboard is also a magnetic board.

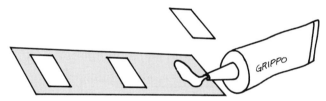

Try using a magnetic board to set up posters or other training material

Charts and posters. Prepared flip charts or posters can be used effectively. With prepared flip charts you may have a lot of standard information that would take too long to write up on a board. With posters you may find that there is something printed that directly relates to the specified subject. When you are finished using these items, remove them before they become a distraction to the group.

Handouts. Handouts are an ideal training aid if we use them correctly. Don't give your handouts to the participants at the beginning of the session unless you want them to read the notes right away. If you want the participants to work through the notes with you, tell them as you give them out. It's common for the handouts to be given at the end of the session.

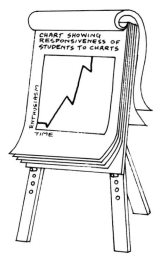

Flip charts can be prepared long before the training session

If the handout covers most of your presentation, tell the participants at the beginning of the session. This practice will allow the participants to give you their undivided attention, as they won't have to make their own notes.

Tape recorders. These are not commonly used in training because most trainers say that a trainee will not sit and listen to a tape recording, but it is up to the trainer to use this training aid effectively. It doesn't always have to be a tape of someone speaking. What about using it for sound effects, or

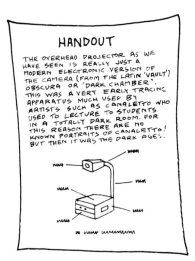

Printed handouts can save the trainees a lot of time

Even the most basic equipment can be effective as a training aid if it is used imaginatively

playing music? If we're to give a presentation on Tchaikovsky, wouldn't a prerecorded tape of Tchaikovsky's Symphony No. 6 in B minor be applicable? (Perhaps it could be used as an introduction.)

Slides. A slide presentation can be used as an excellent break from the routine. Slides are easy to plan and keep up to date but as you do need a darkened room with a slide show, keep it brief. It's also possible to use a slide/tape presentation. A recorded sound tape is used and is synchronised with a series of slides. This allows the trainer to plug in, push the button and enjoy the presentation or pass additional comments over the top of the narrator. The slide/tape presentation does require special equipment to prepare and to play back.

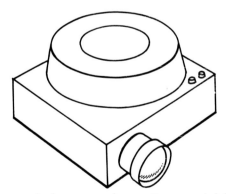

Slide presentations can be kept up to date easily, or varied for different groups

Let's look briefly at some of the advantages and disadvantages of the training aids discussed.

Overhead projector

Advantages: Lets the speaker face the group at all times
Instant placement or removal of information
May be used in normal lighting conditions

Disadvantages: Costly to purchase
Bulky to transport between locations
Requires extra preparation

Films

Advantages: Most are professionally produced
Visually dynamic and portray action
Overcomes the problem of inaccessible places

Disadvantages: Tend to be quickly outdated
Expensive to purchase
Need to be used in dim light

Videos

Advantages: Most are professionally produced
Can be used under normal lighting conditions
Generally can be hired on a short term

Disadvantages: Can be expensive to purchase
Require special equipment for use
Different types of format

Chalkboards

Advantages: Inexpensive to purchase
Consumables easy to obtain
Can use a variety of colours

Disadvantages: Tends to get messy on hands and clothes
Not available in all locations
May require a lot of prework

Whiteboards

Advantages: Generally portable
Consumables easy to obtain
Can use a variety of colours

Disadvantages: Expensive to purchase
Pens dry out quickly
Slippery to write on (unless practised)

Feltboards
Advantages: Inexpensive to make
                   Easy to make portable
                   Can use existing artwork and can be reused
Disadvantages: Not common
                   Wind can blow artwork off board
                   Some people think it's for children

Magnetic boards
Advantages: Relatively inexpensive
                   Able to use existing artwork and can be reused
                   Can be improvised if needed (use a filing cabinet)
Disadvantages: Not common
                   Magnets lose their magnetism
                   Some people think they are for children

Charts and posters
Advantages: Improved colour and quality
                   Easy to carry around
                   Allows material to be prepared and reused
Disadvantages: Tend to damage easily
                   May become a distraction if not moved
                   May require a lot of prework

Handouts
Advantages: Inexpensive to produce
                   Can provide background material not covered
                   A permanent reference for trainees
Disadvantages: May require a lot of prework
                   Can be a distraction if not timed properly
                   May contradict what the speaker is saying

Tape recorders
Advantages: Tapes inexpensive to purchase
                   Very portable
                   Adds variety to the presentation
Disadvantages: May require a lot of prework
                   Cannot be used too often
                   Player system may be expensive

Slides

Advantages: Simple to use and high entertainment value
                     Trainer able to set the pace
                     Easy to edit to bring up to date or alter

Disadvantages: Time consuming to produce
                     Requires darkened room
                     Cannot show motion

Essentials for good visual aids

They need to be simple and easy to understand.
They need to be brief and concise.
They need to stress essential points.
They need to be the correct size and clearly visible.
They need to be interesting.
They should have the right colors, spacing, etc.
They must be applicable to the subject.

Conclusion

Not only do training aids make the learning process easier, they make it more enjoyable. Don't be afraid of applying creativity to your courses. Don't be afraid to adopt someone else's ideas, either, it is a compliment after all.

We can see that there are a great number of training aids available and a good trainer has a working knowledge of all of them. Use as many of them as possible so that you're familiar with all of them. You never know when you may have to fill in for someone else who uses different types of aids.

Training aids improve learning significantly if they're used with imagination and contain relevant information.

Training aids assist us in communicating our knowledge and ideas to the trainee. We should continually be looking at ways to improve or update our training aids. We could also think about combining some of our aids if necessary.

All of our training aids must be presented with a sense of purpose. The trainee must be able to see the purpose and relevance.

The trainer who is always looking for new ways to communicate probably uses training aids creatively

Possibly one of the best training aids we have is the trainee. We haven't discussed the possibility of using the trainee as a training aid. How do you think you could use them effectively?

Further reading

Craig, Robert, *Training and Development Handbook*, 2nd edn, McGraw-Hill Book Company, New York, 1976, Chapter 43.

Dowling, J. R. & Drolet, R. P., *Developing and Administering an Industrial Training Program*, CBI Publishing, Massachusetts, 1979, Part 2.

Goad, Tom, *Delivering Effective Training*, University Associates, California, 1982, Chapter 6.

Laird, Dugan, *Approaches to Training and Development*, Addison-Wesley Publishing Company, Massachusetts, 1978, Chapter 13.

CHAPTER 21

The overhead projector

The overhead projector is becoming one of the most popular forms of training aids in use today and for this reason we will devote a whole chapter to it.

Overhead projectors are now found in most training rooms and conference venues. If the facility cannot supply an overhead projector we can always take one with us from our base. This means, too, that we don't have to rely on proper training or conference rooms. All we have to do is find a location with a power outlet and a light coloured wall to project onto. This isn't an ideal situation, but it would probably be better than nothing.

Most trainers have their own prepared overhead transparencies for any type of presentation they need to give. Trainers find them ideal in most cases as they are compact and durable. A lot of prepared training packages that we can now purchase have overhead transparencies supplied with them, as well as a session plan stating when they should be used.

By using prepared overhead transparencies we can both strengthen and shorten our presentation.

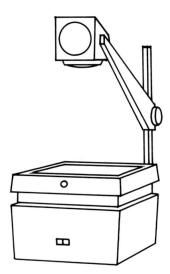

Transparencies for the overhead projector can be prepared well in advance of the session

156

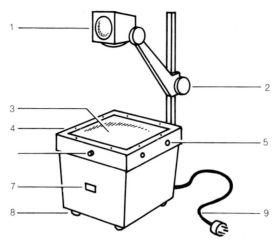

1. Projection head/lens   4. Locating pins for cardboard frames   7. On/off switch
2. Focusing knob   5. Screws for roll feed attachments   8. Levelling legs
3. Fresnel lense/top plate   6. Top plate catch   9. Power cord

The competent trainer knows how all the training aids function

The parts of an overhead projector

Trainers should make sure that they understand the functions of the different parts of an overhead projector (see the diagram above).

There are different types of overhead projectors around. Some are fixed units, some are fold-up units and some have built-in spares. However you will find that they are all similar in their basic design. Check which type you have or will be using.

Where do we use it?

It's usual to have the overhead projector set up in front of the room. When positioning the equipment, ensure that everyone in the audience will be able to see the screen. If you have an adjustable stand to place the overhead projector on, you may adjust it right down so that people who are seated can see over the top of it.

Make sure that none of your training aids obscure the trainees' view

Ideally the stand used for the overhead projector will have enough room on the side to hold your session notes and prepared transparencies.

The projection should be aimed reasonably high on the wall so there is little chance of anyone not being able to see. Unfortunately this may result in a distorted image, wider at the top than the bottom. This distortion is commonly referred to as keystoning. To overcome this keystoning effect we need to use an angled screen. The screen may be angled using wall brackets or if we are using a normal rollup projection screen we can get attachments to make the screen tilt.

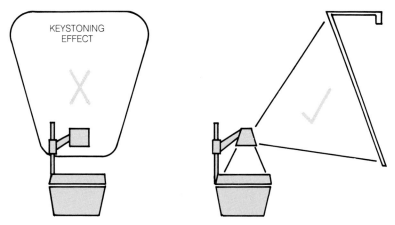

An overhead projector needs an angled screen if the image is being projected well above head level

Making transparencies

The blank transparencies are normally purchased separately or in boxes of 100. There are different colours, sizes and thicknesses. Check with your supplier to find out what will be best for your needs. The transparencies are also referred to by some people as 'acetates', 'slides' or 'foils'.

The first thing we need to do when making an overhead transparency is to work out what information we want to project. When we first start out as trainers we have the temptation to include everything we possibly can on the transparency. Don't fall into this trap. An overhead transparency should only contain key words, phrases or diagrams. The most you want to put on a transparency would be five or six lines of writing with six or seven words in each line. That's not much, so make sure it is effective.

When we know what we want to put on our transparency, we need to lay it out so that it looks presentable. It's best to do a rough pen-and-paper layout so that we know what it should look like. When designing the layout, leave a 2 to 3 centimetre-wide border around the edges. Now that we know what we want to include, and what the layout should look like, we can start on the final version.

There are two basic ways of making the final transparency. The first way is to lay the transparency in front of us and draw what we want using either permanent or water soluble overhead projection pens. Make sure that your lettering is large enough and legible for all to see and read. When you first start producing overheads allow for a couple of trial ones so that you can get the feel of it.

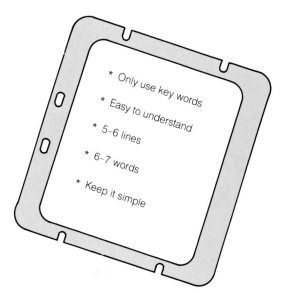

Neat and clear presentation is an important part of any written or diagrammatic training material

Using a permanent overhead projection pen means that what we put on the transparency is permanent. If we use water soluble projection pens it allows us to erase any or all of the artwork easily. Each has its own advantages and disadvantages. If you do use water soluble pens though, be aware that they wipe off easily. You may walk into a training session with blank transparencies as a result of paper rubbing on them. Both types of pen are available in a wide range of colours and thicknesses.

There are also a number of other lettering systems and machines available on the market. However, they are generally expensive and tend to be available only in large organisations that have big training budgets.

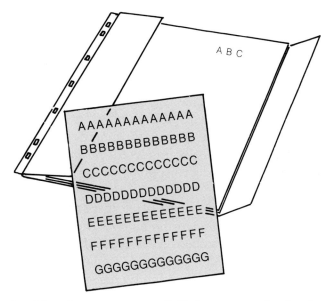

Commercially produced lettering systems are available for use on overhead projector transparencies

The second common way of making overhead transparencies is to use a photocopier. This is an extremely fast method. Check to make sure that your photocopier will accept transparencies. Transparencies that are suitable for photocopiers will be noted on the box. Take your blank transparencies and place them in the paper carrier tray in place of the photocopier paper.

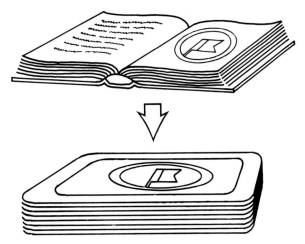

Photocopiers can often be used to create transparencies quickly and effectively

Put your master on the copy screen and push the button. All going well you now have your final product. You can produce overheads of almost anything (including photographs and publications) using this method. It also allows for a cut, paste and copy production. If you have an enlarging facility on your machine you may like to make use of it.

The only slight drawback with this method is that you are normally limited to black printing on your transparency. To make it more interesting, or to highlight the really important points, you may wish to add a bit of color by using overhead projection pens or by using color adhesive film.

You may see continuous rolls of transparency film being used occasionally. The roll is attached to the side of the overhead projector and wound across the projection screen. This type of presentation is not very common as it's extremely difficult to alter or update material and usually all of the artwork for the roll has to be done by hand.

After the single-sheet transparency has been produced it may be mounted in a cardboard frame or a flip frame. With either of these methods we are able to write notes on the side of the frame.

One of the few problems with the cardboard frame is that it's too large to fit in most folders or in a brief case. The flip frame, on the other hand, is not much bigger than the transparency itself. It also has punched holes down one side for use in a ring folder. It can therefore be kept alongside with your session plans with everything in one place and in the correct sequence.

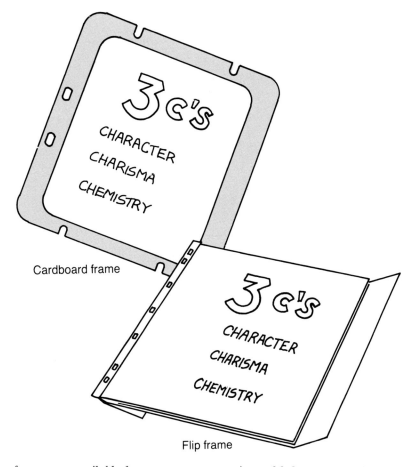

Cardboard frame

Flip frame

Different frames are available for use on transparencies and help to protect them from damage

Let's now look at some more advanced types or designs of overhead transparencies.

Overlay method

Start with a base transparency and keep adding information to it by overlaying other transparencies on top. This is good to use to show how things are constructed or how things go together.

The overlay method allows the trainer to build up a total picture gradually

Write on as you use method

Use your original transparency as a starting point and build to it by writing additional information while you use it. This would be useful for showing how forms are filled in. Use a water soluble pen so that you are able to reuse the transparency.

Write on the transparencies to add extra information as the session progresses

Disclosure methods

Using a disclosure method allows us to reveal certain sections of the overhead transparency as they are required. Methods vary from scrap pieces of paper to hinged pieces of board and can become quite involved.

A quick tip if you use a sheet of paper in the disclosure method. Place your masking sheet under the transparency. This allows you to see what is written without sliding the paper too far and perhaps giving more information than required.

Parts of the transparency can be disclosed gradually as the trainer moves to new information

Tips for using the overhead projector and transparencies

- Check the focus before the presentation starts
- When placing the overhead transparency on the projector, place it the right way up so that you can read it while looking at the audience
- Place the transparency squarely on the top plate
- Ensure the projector is level so that the cooling fan operates at optimum level
- Don't switch the projector off completely until the cooling fan stops
- Keep eye contact with the audience, don't look at the screen
- Turn the projector off when changing transparencies
- Use a pointer on the transparency to show details
- Mask sections of the transparency not required (revealing techniques)
- Turn the projector off when talking of something different to that being projected
- Don't leave the projector turned on for extended periods
- Have all of your transparencies in the correct order
- Let the projector cool down before moving
- Have a spare globe handy (some machines have spare globes built in and can be operated from a switch on the unit)
- Don't place your hands on the glass or lenses
- Don't clean lenses with solvents, you may melt them. Use a soft tissue soaked in warm soapy water
- Practise with the projector before using (some are slightly different from others)
- The projector can also be used to silhouette items, keys, etc.
- Use colours on your transparencies for greater interest
- Keep transparencies simple and legible
- Have the overhead projector serviced regularly

Conclusion

The overhead projector is fast becoming a standard piece of equipment for the professional trainer. As all professional trainers become familiar with the overhead projector, only the best users will be remembered.

To be best you will need to practise with the equipment until you feel as comfortable with it as you do with your best friend.

The new trainer has only to follow the information supplied here on the use of the overhead projector and on the production of overhead transparencies. With that as a base they will probably find that they know as much, if not more, than the professional trainer now does. Proficiency indicates professionalism, so become proficient.

Practice and sound preparation will make you proficient in the use of the overhead projector

Further reading

Minor, E., *Handbook for Preparing Visual Media*, 2nd edn, McGraw-Hill Book Company, New York, 1978.

CHAPTER 22

Contract learning

Contract learning, or self-directed learning, is a relatively new concept to both trainers and learners. It doesn't follow the normal learning procedures that most people are used to. It has a lot of advantages over traditional classroom style learning where participants may just sit and perhaps occasionally listen to, or become involved in, your presentation.

Contract learning lets the learner select the topics or competencies they want to learn. If the topics are selected by the learner they can't complain at a later date that the course work was not relevant to their needs.

The learner can also relate the learning process directly to their own work location or to their required duties. This means that the learner can select tasks that will have meaningful work-related outcomes rather than being an answer to a trainer-designed situation.

Another advantage of contract learning is that the learner contributes to the total design of the learning process. They have to write their own objectives, determine what work is going to be done, determine what resources are going to be used and design the evaluation criteria.

As so much is designed and written by the learner, they really do own the project. This sense of ownership gives them the motivation to carry the project or contract through to the finish.

The whole process is based on *andragogy*, which is the study of how adults learn. A simplistic explanation of andragogy is that adults see themselves as self-directed in their learning as they have had some life experience. This is opposed to children, who expect to be told what they need to do.

Adults have lots of individual differences and these differences increase with life experiences. Adult training, therefore, has to make maximum provision for differences in time, style and learning speed.

The really interesting thing here is that not only do adults appear to learn faster and better using self-directed learning techniques, but, compared with the results of conventional techniques, they learn more deeply and permanently.

What is contract learning?

Contract learning involves a student, participant or learner establishing that they have one or more competencies that need to be raised to a higher level of expertise. With this need established the learner enters into a learning contract, or agreement, with a trainer, facilitator, teacher or adviser.

A number of trades and professions have specific competencies designed and in such cases it is a matter of working through the competencies that need to be addressed by the learner. The learner must agree that their level of expertise needs to be increased. If the level of expertise is currently at a satisfactory level, the competency doesn't need to be followed through.

Trainees can set their own goals when they engage in contract learning

With the base competencies agreed on it then becomes a matter of deciding and agreeing on objectives, resources, proof of goals, evaluation methods and criteria.

It is almost possible that contract learning could be totally learner-based and the whole process could be carried out without an instructor or adviser. However the problem with a totally self-directed package is that there is no-one to check the administration and keep the learner in line with the contract. It's very easy for the learner not to establish a sound contract or to become side-tracked.

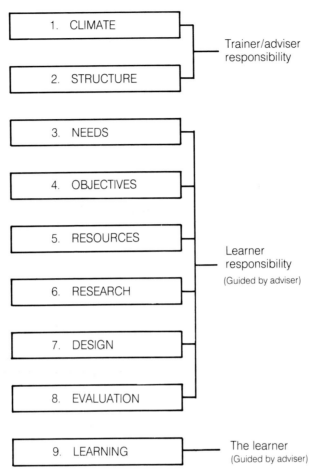

The nine stages of a contract, showing responsibilities

What does a contract look like?

A learning contract is basically a written agreement between a learner and an adviser. There are a number of styles being used at present. A contract similar to the one that I have been successfully using is on the opposite page.

Filling in the contract

Before we fill in a learning contract we need to have identified a competency, so let's assume that has been done. The first step in filling in the contract is to write specific learning objectives. These objectives must state what the learner will learn, not what they will be doing.

Secondly, the contract writer must determine what resources or strategies could be used in meeting the stated needs of the objectives. These could

STUDENT _____	COMPETENCY _____ _____		DATE COMMENCED _/_/_
ADVISOR _____	_____		DATE DUE _/_/_
1. LEARNING OBJECTIVES	2. RESOURCES STRATEGIES	3. WHAT IS TO BE ASSESSED?	4. HOW IS IT TO BE ASSESSED?
This is where all of the learning objectives are written. More than one objective should be designed by the learner. The objectives must be easy to understand and must describe the learning not the doing.	All resources and strategies should be listed here. Not only should books and films be included here, but human resources could also be listed. There may also be a number of other items that need to be carried out by the learner: they should also be included here.	The things that are being assessed should relate directly to the stated learning objectives. However here we are normally looking at what has been done. It could include reports, essays, video tapes, diary details, situations, etc.	Assessment could state the length of the report or essay. It could include a time frame for a video presentation. It could also state that certain experts must agree with the results and the process by which they were achieved. Did the trainer/adviser consider the resources to be used effectively?

(please note that these are only suggestions, anything can be included as long as both the learner and the trainer/adviser agree to the relevance and appropriateness)

APPROVED YES/NO DATE _____/___/_____ ADVISER'S SIGNATURE _____

LEARNER'S SIGNATURE _____

include such things as speaking to subject experts, watching nominated films or videos, reading specific literature, or using any other suitable resource.

Next, the learner must establish what the adviser is to assess. This section of the contract would include items of evidence like essays, reports, projects, problem-solving situations, video-taped presentations, rating scales or anything else that the players can see.

In the fourth column the measurement criteria is established. It may specify that reports are to be of a certain length, videos are to reflect certain standards, reports or essays are to be reviewed by nominated experts for approval and material designed is to be submitted to other experts for approval. More generally, it may simply be a check that the people involved in the case agree that the need has been met.

With the four columns completed the learner reviews the contract with the adviser. The review will include the adviser checking the objectives, checking the resources, checking what is to be assessed and how it is to be assessed on completion. The learner and adviser then negotiate a completion date for the whole project.

The adviser will want to pose some specific questions for all learning contracts while checking them. These questions may include some of the following:

- Are the learning objectives clear?
- Do the objectives relate to what is to be learnt, not done?
- Are the resources and strategies appropriate?
- Are there any other resources that might be useful?
- Are the proposed uses of the resources suitable?
- Are the items being assessed suitable for this contract?
- Are the assessment criteria appropriate?
- Can the learner think of any other form of assessment?
- Are the criteria for assessment fair?
- Should additional criteria be used?
- Has a marking or grading system been established?
- Are the findings going to be presented to the group?

Trainees who are actively involved in devising their own learning program feel a sense of ownership of the ideas

It's important to remember that if you see anything that needs to be modified, you should endeavour to get the learner to recognise the problem and get them to offer suggestions for its improvement. By doing this you are allowing them to keep their ownership of ideas.

Who can use a learning contract?

Using learning contracts in the correct manner allows the learner to experiment with real situations rather than always looking at the theory and at hypothetical cases.

We all learn at different rates. The concept of learning contracts is that the learner decides the pace they want, or need, to set and this pace is always checked with an adviser. The trainer then doesn't have to worry about keeping the faster learners occupied, or how to get the slower ones to catch up.

Learning contracts help to solve the problems associated with the differences in educational backgrounds, life experiences, personal interests, job experiences, different forms of motivation and general abilities of the individuals.

It's important to realise that, regardless of who is using the learning contract, the trainer or adviser must enlist the active participation of the learner if the process is to work properly.

No matter who uses learning contracts we can say that the learners all take the initiative for learning. They don't simply sit and become involved in a one-way communication.

Conclusion

Learning contracts are used to design learning experiences; they are not a learning process in themselves. They must be used effectively for maximum benefit to the learner and to the trainer.

At the beginning of any self-directed learning situation the trainer must design the process to involve early participation of the learner. This serves two purposes; it sets the scene for the learner and it allows for maximum input by the learner.

Adults generally request immediate and relevant application of what they are learning and contract learning gives them this.

What is going to happen to the trainer, lecturer, teacher or presenter? Will they become a thing of the past? I don't think so. Their roles will be modified to include a managing or guiding of the andragogic learning process. This modification will call for more negotiation and facilitation skills.

Contract learning will be one of the learning processes of the future, for both young and old.

Application example

I have two situations for you to look at in this chapter. Firstly let's look at the typical adolescent schooling process. In this situation we tend to always have the knowledgable teacher and the student who is lacking information.

In contrast to this if we look at an adult education facility we normally see trainers who have expertise in one main area and students who have expertise in other areas. The trainer in this case will generally build in a knowledge or experience network of resources for all of the students to use.

In other words, the trainer is allowing the individuals to share their own life experiences with the group. Although this doesn't directly have anything to do with contract learning it indicates the possibility of self-directed learning.

I would like to share with you a past experience with contract learning. Previously I attended a college that used self-directed contract learning.

Although it took a while to get used to setting my own learning objectives, I found it very satisfying. Part of this book was actually written as the result of my learning contracts. A number of chapters in this book were originally designed as learning contracts, submitted, modified and approved by my adviser.

It's interesting to note that until becoming involved with learning contracts I had never been interested in writing or having anything published, but as the result of my own motivation, or the sense of owning the ideas, it makes it easy to study, research and write.

I couldn't complain about the competencies selected or any of my learning objectives because I had decided what they needed to be at the very beginning of my attendance.

If I identified new areas that I needed to research, it was then a matter of writing up some new contracts and submitting them for approval. (They only need to be approved to gain credits for the work done.)

So all of the points I have covered in this chapter actually did occur with our learning contracts. One very interesting point is that a number of the trainees attending the course are doing far more work than is required for the course. It's this in-built motivation that keeps us going in a positive direction.

It really does work!

Further reading

Howes, Virgil, *Individualisation of Instruction*, Macmillan Publishing, New York, 1970.

Knowles, Malcolm, *Self-directed Learning*, Cambridge, New York, 1975.

Knowles, Malcolm, *The Adult Learner. A Neglected Species*, 2nd edn., Gulf Publishing Company, Houston, 1978.

CHAPTER 23

Budgets

This section isn't going to turn you into a financial whiz. What it will do is give you an insight into what the Training Manager has to allow for, financially, each year. It should also let you know why the Training Manager sometimes carries a crystal ball around the office.

Every department of an organisation has to prepare a budget. But when preparing a budget for training, we generally do not know in advance what problems we have to fix, or what some of the training gaps are that we have to fill.

The only time Training Managers know in advance of the problems that are going to arise in the organisation, is if they are invited to participate in the decisions of the company. This is how Training Managers should operate, but unfortunately they don't, or are not allowed to in many cases.

The complexity of the training budget normally reflects the attitude of senior management. If the training section is merely a token division, the budget does not normally need to be too large or too detailed because the organisation has already decided on what appropriation the section is going to get. At the end of the year they probably will not have to show performance either.

If the organisation is really committed to training, much more information will be required. What they want to know most importantly is whether or not the training is going to be cost-effective. Most organisations

Training budgets can sometimes be difficult to calculate

are interested in showing some financial profit for the shareholders. However in most situations the training budget needs to be reasonably detailed so that it is possible to accurately predict the cost of training.

What is a budget?

A budget is a list of expenses the training section is expected to be billed for over a given period of time, which is generally twelve months. These expenses are all associated with the cost of training within the organisation.

The budget is not one-sided. The organisation does not possess the legendary money tree. The training section cannot just say how much money they need and expect the money to be allocated to them without question.

What happens after the expected costs have been established by the training section is that the Training Manager has to negotiate with the senior management of the organisation so that they all get what they require.

To justify its expenses, the training section needs to be able to state whether or not the organisation is going to get a return on its investment in training.

When these expenses, or costs, have been agreed to by the senior management, it's up to the Training Manager to ensure that they aren't exceeded.

A training budget is very similar in principle to a household budget. Usually the house-spouse requests a certain amount of money each pay day; this amount is an estimate of what they expect, or need, to spend before the next pay day.

The salary earner may then question what the money is to be spent on, and what they are going to get for it. Only if there is a sufficient amount of money available, and the salary earner can see that they are going to get value for their money, will the full amount requested be handed over. Often there are not sufficient funds available and the house-spouse has to compromise. That's the negotiation period.

It doesn't matter, for the purposes of this exercise, whether the full amount of the initial request, or the new negotiated figure, was handed over. What does matter is that regardless of the amount given, the house-spouse must stick to the original or revised estimates. When the money runs out, there is no more.

This type of situation may also involve the training section in setting priorities for the money to be spent. The priorities need to be set in case the funds allocated cannot cover all the training required. If the funds aren't

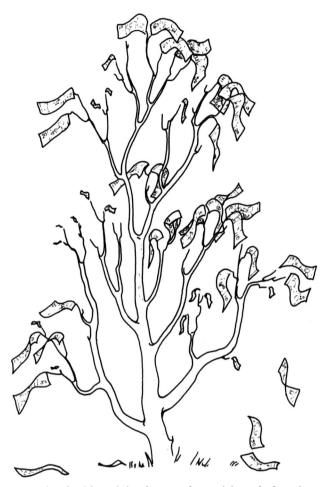

The expenses associated with training have to be anticipated; there is no money tree

sufficient it's a matter of dropping, or postponing, the training programme with the lowest priority, assuming that we can't change our methods of training to something less costly. Whatever the amount, it must be spent wisely and the section should be able to justify its expenses.

Estimating training costs

We don't know exactly how much it will cost us, but we can estimate very accurately how much training 'things' are going to cost us over a specified period of time. This estimate of costs is our budget once it's approved by management.

To estimate what training we may have to do the Training Manager will need to be involved with other sections within the organisation. They should also be involved in the decisions being made by senior management. This involvement is necessary so that the Training Manager knows in advance about proposed changes to the organisational structure, proposed changes to production, changes in technology which may involve retraining, and many other areas.

When we know what training will be needed, we can look at the separate components and estimate how much each component will cost. Some of these components could be things like the cost of trainers' wages, the cost of printing, the cost of venue hire, and many other components.

How is the course cost broken down?

The course cost can be broken down into three main parts: preparation costs, direct course costs and administration costs.

Firstly we have the preparation costs such as typing costs, phone expenses, course design costs and other precourse expenses.

Secondly there are direct course costs, those directly associated with the training programme. They would include the expense of trainers' wages, trainees' wages, venue costs, consultant costs, meals, accommodation, consumable items and any cost that is related the learning of the programme.

Lastly we have the administrative costs. Administrative costs would include trainers' wages for the evaluation of the course, transport costs, hire costs, handouts, booklets, pens, paper, folders and general office overheads.

If we use these groups we can be reasonably certain that we're going to cover all of the items that we need to in our estimates.

What to budget for

We should obviously budget for all of the anticipated training courses that we will be conducting over the budget period. We must also budget for other standard running costs such as the purchase of new equipment, upgrading equipment, software, maintenance, stationery, consumable items, advertising, consultancy time with management, training of trainers, training management and support staff wages and anything else that we will have to pay for which is not going to be costed directly to the training programs.

When we try to estimate how much the problem is worth, we might also look at the long-term costs of recruiting new staff, the costs of transfering someone, the costs associated with training a person to do a new job, the costs of terminating a person's employment, and many other long-term costs which you may not have thought of before.

Will training be worthwhile?

One of the major problems with training departments is that some of them don't take the time to evaluate the training programs after they have finished. If training managers evaluated the programs properly, they may find they can produce evidence of their successes and may not find negotiations so difficult next time. By evaluating your training courses you can also report back to management on how cost-effective the training program had been. They want to know if they're going to get a return on their investment.

When we forecast the total cost of the program it may indicate that we can fix the problem cost-effectively if we can find a more inexpensive way to carry out the training. If we find that the training program is going to cost more than the problem, it would be wise to redirect those funds to a more cost-effective program.

The only times when the training department should take on a training course that is not going to be cost-effective is when they are directed to do so by management, or if the problem is creating too much tension within the organisation. With the latter situation, it's possible to work out the cost of tension to the organisation if we think about it. Tension can be costly to the organisation in staff turnover, loss of clients, increased accident rates,

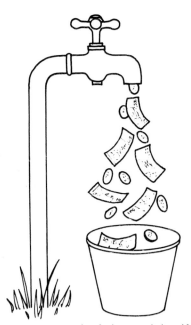

The company is unlikely to pour extra funds into training if the budget has been exceeded

loss of profits and many other areas. If the training staff have the resources they can accurately establish the cost of any identified problem.

However to take on a training programme that is going to cost more than the identified problem, we must be directed by management to do so.

Conclusion

If training has been proven by the training department to be cost-effective, we have a much greater chance of the training budget being accepted by the senior management of the organisation.

Before we can be reasonably certain that the proposed training budget will be totally accepted, we need to be absolutely positive that the organisation will be investing money in something that they will be getting a return on.

The training budget must look ahead, allow for contingencies, set priorities, be coordinated, be accurate, contain sufficient detail and should have the input of all staff involved in training.

Once the budget has been set and agreed to, it's up to the training department to stay within the constraints set. Some form of monitoring system should be designed to allow for this. Unfortunately we can't just turn on a tap and have money flow out of it.

Application example

An application example for this chapter would be far too complex. As you may imagine it would take dozens of pages, and then might not be applicable to your needs. What you now need to do, is to go to your Training Manager and ask if you may have a look at the training budget for your organization.

After you are familiar with the contents, ask how some of the estimates were achieved. If you feel inclined to find out more about training budgets,

See if you can find out how your company arrives at its training budget

why not ask if you can assist next time the training budget needs to be prepared? If you do volunteer for a task like that, make sure you use your crystal ball properly. You may find that some of the forms shown here will be of assistance.

PROGRAM CHECKLIST			
Prepared by: _____			
Co-ordinator: _____			
Item	*Date required*	*Date completed*	*Done by*
Book venue			
Confirm speakers			
Order support materials			
Confirm hire arrangements			
Send memo for nominations			
Send memo to participants			
Send memo to participants' supervisors			
Book travel requirements			
Book accommodation			
Meal arrangements			
Order folders and stationery			
Order consumables			
Typing completed			
Printing completed			
Send out precourse materials			
Confirm participants by phone			
Confirm speakers by phone			
Confirm travel arrangements			
Pick up films, videos, etc.			
Pick up hire items			
Prepare training room			
Participant records noted			
Evaluation			
Certificates			
Written report on program			
Other			

Sample forms

TRAINER COSTING FORM								
Name: _____ Week trained: _____								
Program	Mon	Tue	Wed	Thur	Fri	Sat	Sun	Total hours
Daily totals								

COURSE BUDGET FORM			
COURSE TITLE: _____			
DATES: _____			
LOCATION: _____			
BUDGET PREPARED BY: _____			
ITEM	BUDGET	ACTUAL	NOTES
PREPARATION COSTS SALARIES: TRAINERS 　　　　DESIGNERS 　　　　TYPIST 　　　　CONSULTANT 　　　　CO-ORDINATOR 　　　　　OFFICE SUPPORT 　　　　STAFF 　　　　　MANAGEMENT 　　　　　MEETING 　　　　ALLOWANCES 　　　PHONE CALLS 　　　MAIL COSTS 　　　STATIONERY 　　　PRINTING 　　　ARTWORK 　　PHOTOCOPYING PREPARED TRAINING MATERIALS SPECIAL EQUIPMENT NEEDED 　　MISCELLANEOUS			
DIRECT COURSE COSTS SALARIES: TRAINERS 　　　　TRAINEES 　　　　RELIEF STAFF 　　　　CONSULTANT 　　　　OTHER SPEAKERS 　　　　CO-ORDINATOR 　　　　　MANAGEMENT 　　　ALLOWANCES TRAVEL (TO & FROM) 　　VEHICLE HIRE 　　　MEALS 　ACCOMMODATION 　　BAR CHARGES 　　EVALUATION 　TRANSPORTATION 　　VENUE HIRE 　EQUIPMENT HIRE CONSUMABLE ITEMS 　　BREAKAGES 　PHOTOCOPYING 　MISCELLANEOUS			
ADMINISTRATION COSTS SALARIES: EVALUATORS 　　ALLOWANCES 　　TRANSPORT 　HIRE OF FILMS, ETC 　　HANDOUTS 　　BOOKLETS PENS, PAPER, FOLDERS 　　STATIONERY 　　　FEES 　PHONE, FAX, TELEX 　　INSURANCE 　OFFICE OVERHEADS			

Further reading

Baird, L., Schneier, C. & Laird, D., *The Training and Development Sourcebook*, Human Resource Press, Massachusetts, 1985, Part 1, Section IX, C.

Craig, Robert, *Training and Development Handbook*, 2nd edn, McGraw-Hill Book Company, New York, 1976, Chapter 4.

Laird, Dugan, *Approaches to Training and Development*, Addison-Wesley Publishing Company, Massachusetts, 1978, Chapter 14.

Poulter, Bruce, *Training and Development*, CCH Australia Limited, Australia, 1982, pp 801–8.

CHAPTER 24

Multiculturalism in training

Training in a multicultural society is more than just an interesting experience or change of pace. By dealing with people from other cultures it allows us to draw on new participant experiences. This can have the effect of not only making it more interesting for you, but more interesting for the other participants, particularly if the experiences are meaningful to the group as a whole.

Training in a multicultural society recognises the demographic composition of society and its diversity of cultures and languages.

Multicultural training isn't something that can be ignored. Most countries are now planning for increased numbers of overseas-born residents in their staff numbers and in their training rooms.

Most trainers will find that a large percentage of their groups have been born overseas or come from different cultures. These percentages will continue to grow.

To assist new trainers when they are presenting to a group of mixed cultures, I have listed a few pointers to be followed.

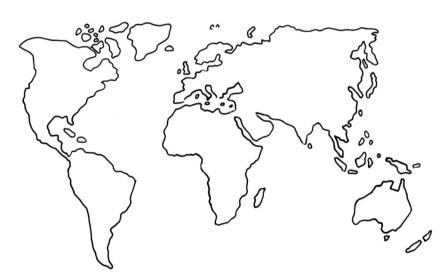

Trainers frequently find that many members of their groups are born overseas

- Speak clearly and pause occasionally.
  Not 'Gizalookatyareport',
  but 'Can I have a look at your report?'
- Frequently check understanding, but avoid yes/no questions.
  Not 'Do you understand?',
  but 'How would you describe it?'
- Don't drop words when speaking, it doesn't help.
  Not 'Put here',
  but 'Put it here.'
- Avoid raising your voice, they're not deaf.
  Not yelling to get the message through,
  but speaking in a normal voice.
- Give notice when you're changing topics.
  Not just carrying on,
  but 'Now we've completed that, let's go on to . . .'
- Don't use sarcastic remarks, they may be misunderstood.
  Not 'Sure it is' (said sarcastically),
  but 'I don't think that's right.'
- Use simple everyday words
  Not 'A philatelist',
  but 'A person who collects stamps.'
- Avoid complicated sentences or ideas.
  Not putting numerous ideas together,
  but presenting them one at a time.
- Give instructions in the sequence to be followed.
  Not 'Before you write it see me',
  but 'See me first then write it.'
- Try not to use strings of negatives.
  Not 'You can't do it if you haven't got one of these',
  but 'You need one of these to do it.'
- Use direct questions.
  Not 'You've done it, haven't you?',
  but 'Have you done it yet?'
- Slang and colloquialisms will create confusion.
  Not 'Pull the other one',
  but 'Are you trying to trick me?'
- Be patient.
  Sometimes it takes a lot of time and understanding so you need to be patient.

While it's understood that there are different levels of understanding on the participant's part, I am aiming at a training situation where all of the participants are reasonably fluent in the trainer's language, but who occasionally come across some stumbling blocks in communication or learning.

The list of pointers just given is also relevant for use with participants who speak your language but with a different accent. Sometimes it's just assumed that a participant who speaks your language will understand you. Experienced travellers and trainers will tell you, correctly, that this is not the case, and these situations may, in fact, be more of a problem than we are generally aware of.

Our participants' learning habits have been developed from their schooling and work experience. These habits will differ from culture to culture, from sub-culture to sub-culture and from individual to individual within the sub-cultures.

While it's easy to say that we should have a knowledge of these participants' learning habits, most of the time it is impractical. It is more practical to say that we should be aware of different learning habits and allow for them in the training room.

It's worth noting that with some languages we are faced with the additional problem of not having technical terms with equivalent meanings. This is something that an international trainer must be aware of. However in most typical training situations the points covered previously will suffice.

If you are placed in a situation where an interpreter is required, make certain that they are a professional interpreter and not just someone who is bilingual. A bilingual translator may not get the correct message across.

If you're going to be training with markedly different cultures or in places where your language may not be understood, it should be obvious that additional training on your part will be required.

Conclusion

As professional trainers we must deal with lots of different situations. The multicultural issues in training have been around for some time, so our employers have a right to expect that we will be able to take control of these situations.

The other point here is that the participants can see us working effectively with these problems and may learn some of our skills by simple observation techniques. This has to be an added benefit to the trainer, the employee and the employer.

Further reading

The issue of multiculturalism in training is a new area of study. Research has shown that not a great deal has been published about it.

Should you require further information on this topic you should contact the relevant government department in your area.

CHAPTER 25

Competency-Based Training

This chapter is intended to give the reader a simple overview of what Competency-Based Training (CBT) is. It is not intended that the reader will become an expert in the design and administration of Competency-Based Training programs from this information.

What is Competency-Based Training?

Let's start by looking at what Competency-Based Training or Competency-Based Education is. There may be more than one interpretation for these terms. However, looking at the varying definitions given one could safely assume that it is meant to mean something like 'an educational process that is based on specific competencies that have been previously identified'.

Competency-Based Training is a way of globally approaching vocational training that has a its main focus on what the person can actually do in the workplace as a result of the training. It is concerned with training to industry-specific standards rather than with the individual's achievement in comparison to others in the group. Or simply, can they do it or not?

When we look at a traditional time-based approach to education, we can easily see that if the program has been correctly designed initially, it will meet the same criteria. By traditional time-based education I mean a properly structured training program with clearly defined objectives that are measurable. If they are measurable we can then say that the trainee can or cannot do what they were supposed to be able to do at the conclusion of the training.

Simply stated, if we allow for a larger involvement of different parties in the design of the training objectives, and allow credit for what the trainee previously knew before training, this is what Competency-Based Training is.

What is Recognition of Prior Learning?

Recognition of Prior Learning (RPL) is only a small part of Competency-Based Training. One needs to be aware also that recognition of participants' previous knowledge and skills can also be considered with traditional training programs.

Recognition of Prior Learning is acknowledging the fact that sometimes (most times?) our trainees already know some of what the instruction is about, and therefore allowing them credit for what they have previously learnt. Applying this to its full extent, a person can be awarded certification without ever attending training.

What's the difference between CBT and ordinary training?

The traditional time-based approach to education initially identifies a training or learning need and sets about to fill that need. When the focus is on Competency-Based Training it may appear that the designer identifies only the more easily measurable competencies (simple as opposed to complex competencies).

A Competency-Based Training system is made up of two components. Firstly, there is an instruction aimed at a learner achieving competency in precisely defined skills and knowledge to specified standards and under specific conditions. Secondly, there should be certification based on the correct assessment of competencies achieved off-the-job and on-the-job.

These competencies should be agreed to by all parties involved, that is, training authorities, employer groups, industry groups, trades groups, relevant councils, employee representative groups, employees, etc. This will allow for consistency with outcomes and therefore will allow for more mobility of competencies, both in industry and in location.

How do you develop a CBT program?

There are five major steps in the development of a Competency-Based Training program. These steps are:

1. An extensive consultative process between relevant parties or groups to identify the relevant skills needed for a particular position in a particular industry.
2. The skills that are identified are organized into appropriate groups from which learning activities can be developed.
3. The physical materials that the program will be based on are developed. Sometimes these will be more extensive than those in traditional type training programs.
4. The people administering the Competency-Based Training will need to be trained. Their instructional style may need to be modified to allow more flexibility (but not flexibility of outcomes). These people will also need to become aware of the assessment criteria. This must be consistent.

5. Ways of recording information are identified and established. Generally the administrative component of Competency-Based Training requires far more effort than traditional training programs.

Competency standards

Competency standards provide the specification of the knowledge and skill and the application of that knowledge and skill to the standard of performance required in employment. There are three interrelated types of standards, which are described below.

1. **Industry Standards:** the national competency standards endorsed for a specific industry.
2. **Cross-Industry Standards:** based on competencies common to a range of industries. These are generally used to facilitate portability, consistency and efficiency in the development of standards.
3. **Enterprise Standards:** standards which consist of competencies developed and/or used specifically at enterprise level. They may or may not include Industry or Cross-industry standards.

A competency standard consists of the following format:

- Elements of competency
- Performance criteria
- Range-of-variables statement
- Evidence guide.

Elements of Competency describe actions or outcomes that are demonstrable or assessable. They are written in input and output terms, and in relation to units of competency they are the lowest logical and identifiable sub-groupings of actions and knowledge which contribute to and build a unit.

Performance Criteria are statements that an assessor can use to judge the performance specified in the elements of competence to a level acceptable in employment. The performance criteria must be written to provide a link between the competency and its evidence of achievement.

The **range-of-variables statement** specifies the range of contexts and conditions to which the Performance Criteria apply.

The **evidence guide** is an optimal part of the standard, covering contexts for assessment, critical aspects of a unit, and its relationship to other units and the required evidence of competency.

Conclusion

Competency-Based Training identifies specific outcomes through the involvement of all relevant parties. It improves the mobility of knowledge and skills for the learner.

We need to be aware, however, that Competency-Based Training can sometimes create an extravagant system or number of systems that are expensive in their design, structure and administration. Education needs to more clearly target its resources on an educational process, rather than creating more of a bureaucracy.

Many experts now state that it is an expensive system to design, structure and administer. They also believe that there may be an additional expense in the fact that sometimes the program can be out of date before it is even released! This is sometimes due to the amount of time required to set these programs up.

We need to be aware that Competency-Based Training may, in some cases, settle for mediocrity. It may also overlook the more creative type solutions to some situations. It has also been said that it may not allow for

Competency-Based Training can be expensive in design, structure and administration

perfection. It may not allow for people to excel. Is it acceptable for a person to only solve a problem in one particular way? What if the learner creates a solution that hasn't been written into the assessment of Competency-Based Training? Do they fail? Assessment is a key part of Competency-Based Training.

With Competency-Based Training we need to ensure that the system itself doesn't consume all of the training dollars. It can be a very expensive program.

Application example

An example in the design of a Competency-Based Training program would take up far to much space in a chapter that has been offered as an overview only. If you wish to look at examples in this area I would suggest you obtain some of the publications in the Further Reading list at the end of the chapter which have numerous detailed examples from many different fields.

When looking for examples, try to find ones in areas that you are familiar with.

Further reading

Ashworth, P.D. and Saxton, J., *On Competence*, 1990.

Collins, Roger & Saul, Peter, *Management Competencies Development Program,* McGraw-Hill Book Company, Sydney, 1991.

Confederation of Australian Industry, *CBT: Proposals For the Australian Vocational Educational and Training System*, 1991.

Foyster, John, *Getting To Grips With Competency Based Training and Assessment*, TAFE, South Australia. 1990.

Hager, P., Gonzi, A. & Oliver, L., *Competency Based Approaches to Professional Education*, 1990.

Henerson, Marlene, *How To Measure Attitudes*, Sage Publications, California, 1987.

Klemp, G. O., *Job Competence Assessment: Defining the Attributes of the Top Performer*, 1982.

National Competency Standards, Department of Employment, Education and Training (DEET), 1991.

McDonald, S., *Competency-Based Training Pilot Projects Data Base*, Vocational Educational, Employment and Training Advisory Committee (VEE-TAC), 1991.

Rumsey, D. J. & Hawke, G. A., *Competency-Based Testing—A TAFE Approach*, TAFE, 1988.

TAFE, *Assessing Competency in the Workplace*, Open College Network, Sydney, 1990.

CHAPTER 26

Outdoor-Based Training

What is Outdoor-Based Training?

When referring to Outdoor-Based Training or Outdoor-Based Learning we need to ask ourselves what Outdoor-Based Learning is? What makes it a valuable learning experience? Does it work? And if it does work, how does it work and who for?

> *A furry creature (trainee odoriferous), streaked with dirt, bursts into your office. He places a wooden object resembling a miniature totem pole on top of the new videodisc player you have requisitioned. He drags you out of your chair for a bone-crushing bear hug and declares with wild eyes and panting breath: 'We just got back. I love this kind of training!'*
>
> *Solemnly, almost ritualistically, he presents you with 'Fa', the wooden totem of his clan-team, from the Pole Cats. Fa was lovingly carved with the edge of a dull rock by the light of a campfire while the clan chanted your new corporate mantra. You muster a mumbled thanks, he hugs you again and tromps off, leaving a trail of straw and dirt. As corporate training manager, you dutifully add Fa to the other icons atop your credenza, wisely choosing to give it the most prominent position. After all, this one did come from your CEO.*
>
> *A moment later, another bedraggled soul slumps in peevishly. Ah, you think,* trainee blisterous. *He says what you expect: 'I hated it. You call this training? I didn't learn a thing—except maybe to stay off the pamper pole with tight underwear and bring more bug repellent.' Too bad, you think. This guy is the vice president of human resources—your boss.*

(Thompson, 1991)

Outdoor-Based Learning is any learning activity, exercise or simulation that can be conducted outside the classroom environment—that is, out of the traditional learning environment.

Outdoor-Based Training can be seen as an ongoing professional development program for seasoned executives, or as a resource for meeting the special challenges of transition management during reorganization, or, more commonly, it can be used to improve co-operation, develop trust, improve teams, and build confidence in training groups or work groups etc. Challenges or activities are designed according to desired program outcomes.

196

Outdoor-Based Training can improve co-operation, develop trust, and build confidence

Outdoor-Based Training promotes many team-centred activities and individual development activities. Some of these activities include ropes activities, skirmish, paintball, hangliding, bushwalking, camping, scuba diving, windsurfing, motorsports, skydiving, grass skiing, sailboarding, rollerblading, canoeing, bush trail rides, simulations, and many many others.

There are two distinct types of Outdoor-Based Learning. One is generally referred to as 'Adventure Training' and includes high-risk activities or perceived high-risk activities. The other uses low-risk activities and is generally referred to as 'Outdoor Learning' or 'Outdoor Training'.

Outdoor-Based Learning conjures up many different pictures to many different people.

Where is it used?

Does such high-impact training make any difference in participants' attitudes and work behaviors? Does it affect organizational outcomes? The whole issue is open to question. Many trainers believe this type of training does work, provided the rules for other types of effective training programs are respected. These include clear objectives, skilled facilitation, a plan to transfer the knowledge gained back to the job, and credible evaluation and follow up.

Most Outdoor-Based Training programs are conducted for team initiative and group problem solving exercises. Current research indicates that the objectives for Outdoor Training programs are:

Wilderness programs
Leadership	60%
Decision making	40%

Outdoor-centred programs
Team building	90%
Self-esteem	50%
Leadership	40%
Problem solving	20%
Decision making	15%
Sense of corporate ownership	2%

High-risk and low-risk activities

Outdoor-Based Learning combines cognitive learning with subjective interpretations based on the individuals' feelings, attitudes and values. When we look further into Outdoor-Based Learning programs being conducted, we see that the vast majority of experiential exercises used outdoors are high-risk activities. A generally accepted definition of a high-risk activity is where the participants may be higher than eye-level above the ground during the activity, or have a perceived risk of danger or injury to themselves. Low-risk activities are generally where the participants are no higher than eye-level from the ground or perceive the activity to be almost accident free.

Examples of high-risk activities include orienteering, cross-country navigation, abseiling, white-water rafting, cross-country skiing, zip wires, and high ropes courses. Examples of low-risk activities include simulations such as spider's web, sinking islands, prouty's landing, Australian trolley, and trust walks.

It would appear that most high-risk activities were originally designed to develop the individual, while the lower-risk activities seem to highlight the need for improved teamwork, improved problem solving and decision making skills, and improved communication skills. This is still generally true.

Is there a sequence?

The first attempt at a formal Outdoor-Based Training program took place in 1941. Outdoor programs first began to attract corporate attention around the world in the late 1970s and early 1980s. They have grown dramatically in popularity since then. It can be seen that the start of formal Outdoor-Based Learning did centre on the development of individual skills rather than having a team centred approach. This now seems to have altered.

We still see the focus on the individual when Outdoor-Based Learning is used to develop higher-level leadership skills. While some leadership skills can be developed in a team situation, it is felt that the higher one gets in most organizations, the more individual attention may be required to find or improve these leadership skills.

The four levels of application for Outdoor-Based Training are set out below.

First level Traditional classroom based training activities	Imparts general knowledge and skills required to perform specific duties and tasks.
Second level Lower-risk Outdoor-Based Training activities, incorporating group problem-solving challenges	Targets the development of improved organizational communication. Used to improve co-operation, improve teamwork, and build confidence in specific training groups. *Example activity:* spider's web
Third level Lower-risk Outdoor-Based Training activities, incorporating individual challenges requiring team support	Similar to the second level but far more emphasis on activities requiring team support and developing trust. *Example activity:* trust walk
Fourth level Higher-risk Outdoor-Based Training activities and wilderness programs	Takes on the role of allowing individual participants to discover more about themselves and their relationships with others, to gain new insights into their abilities and potential, to develop self-reliance, resourcefulness and determination to succeed, and to enhance self-motivation and raise personal standards of achievement. *Example activity:* zip wire

The table shows the first level of training as being traditional classroom-based training applications. This level imparts general knowledge and skills required to perform specific duties and tasks. The second level shows the application of lower-risk Outdoor-Based Training. This level targets the development of improved organizational communication. It is used to improve co-operation, improve teamwork, and build confidence in training groups. The third level develops trust within teams. It also develops team support. The fourth level takes on the role of allowing participants to discover more about themselves and their relationships with others, to gain new insights into their abilities and potential, to develop self-reliance resourcefulness and determination to succeed, and to enhance self-motivation and raise personal standards of achievement.

Defining levels in this way is not an attempt to suggest that any one level is better than any other. What it does attempt to do is show the progression of Outdoor-Based Training applications. It would also appear that some organizations and some countries may be operating at different levels, both for the right and wrong reasons.

What makes a good program?

Most successful Outdoor-Based Learning programs have very detailed introductions or orientations at the beginning of the program. They all have thorough debriefings with links back to the workplace or wherever is appropriate.

Outdoor-Based Training programs, like all other programs, need to have clearly defined objectives before commencement of the training. Both trainers and organizations must be conscious of the fact that if not properly designed these programs may have only entertainment value. Poor design could lead to the situation where the participants say they had a good time, when perhaps they didn't really learn anything. In this case, if the only aim you had for the program was for the participants to have a good time, well, then it can be seen as a success.

Another consideration when designing this type of program, is to ensure the correct sequencing of all activities used in any program, regardless of which level. One of the keys to success of any outdoor program is the correct sequence of its activities.

It would appear that there are three ways people change on these programs. They are through shock, through evolution, or through anticipation. Each has its own application. This needs to be considered along with the different levels shown above.

If you put a frog in a pan of hot water he jumps right out, but if you put him in a pan of cold water he just swims around even though you turn the heat up a little by little. He adapts . . . right to frog legs. (Wilson 1987)

Conclusion

To design a highly relevant program, providers must find out exactly what the work group or individual sees as its strengths and weaknesses and what kinds of problems must be addressed.

In addition to this they must ascertain what level of Outdoor-Based Learning activities are best suited to each situation. The outcomes must also be limited to a reasonable one or two, not a fix-all for everything.

Outdoor-Based Training is still a fairly new field and has plenty of room to grow and to demonstrate its strengths. If future programs are designed and implemented correctly, we may have only seen the tip of the iceberg.

Application example

The spider's web

The spider's web is a popular outdoor activity used by facilitators, and can be used to improve teamwork and communication as well as many other skills.

To prepare for this the facilitator must find at least two trees (or poles) and create a spider's web between them, using several lengths of string or wool. This is generally best done by firstly tying two pieces of rope between the two trees. One should be fairly close to ground level and the other at least above eye-level. When finished, it should look something like a spider's web and have enough openings as appropriate for the activity (usually one opening for each participant to fit through).

The facilitator usually sets a problem for the group to solve. One story may be that everyone is trapped in a dark dungeon and the only way to get out is to climb through the spider's web. Unfortunately if anyone touches the web while trying to get through, the spider will feel the vibrations and come and eat everyone. Because of the particular design of this spider's web each opening can only be used once. The facilitator would also mention all of the safety instructions for this activity, such as no running and diving through openings.

Many variations can be incorporated into this activity. One example of that may be in the case when one person takes complete control of the

The spider's web is a popular activity, used to improve teamwork and communication

situation when this is not what the facilitator requires. In this case the facilitator could tell the group that the spider has just seen the group planning to destroy its web and has fired some of its sticky web material toward them. The substance has hit one person in the face and as a result has stuck that persons lips and eyes together! Get the idea? If necessary a time limit can also be imposed on the group.

After the group has completed the activity the facilitator can lead a discussion into the selected topic area. These topic areas could include leadership styles, teamwork, planning, risk-taking, communication skills, roles, synergy, etc.

Like any good outdoor activity, the main value is in the debriefing of the event and the link back to reality.

Further reading

Action Magazine, April 1992.

Ayers, Keith, 'Executives in the Wilderness', *Staff Recruitment, Training & Development*, 1990, 34–7.

Buller, Paul, Cragun, John & McEvoy, Glenn, 'Getting the Most out of Outdoor Training', *Training & Development Journal*, March 1991, 45 (3), 58–61.

Collard, Mark & Thompson, Bill, 'Adventure Approach to Corporate Training', *Training and Development in Australia*, March 1992, 19 (1), 11–13.

Galagan, Patricia, 'Between Two Trapezes', *Training & Development Journal*, March 1987, 41 (3), 40–8.

Gall, Adrienne, 'You Can Take the Managers out of the Woods, but . . .' *Training & Development Journal*, March 1987, 41 (3), 54–8.

Huszczo, Gregory, 'Training for Team Building', *Training & Development Journal*, February 1990, 44 (2), 37–43.

Long, Janet, 'The Wilderness Lab Comes of Age', *Training & Development Journal*, March 1987, 41 (3), 30–9.

Thompson, Brad Lee, 'Training in the Great Outdoors', *Training*, May 1991, 28 (5), 46–52.

Wagner, Richard, Baldwin, Timothy & Roland, Christopher, 'Outdoor Training: Revolution or Fad?', *Training & Development Journal*, March 1991, 45 (3), 51–7.

Wilson, Larry, 'Come to the Ranch and Play the Game', *Training & Development Journal*, March 1987, 41 (3), 49–50.

Zenger, John, Musselwhite, Ed, Hurson, Kathleen & Perrin, Craig, 'Leadership in a Team Environment', *Training & Development*, October 1991, 45 (10), 47–52.

Sources of outdoor activities

Fluegelman, Andrew, *The New Games Book*, Doubleday, New York, 1976.

Fluegelman, Andrew, *More New Games*, Doubleday, New York, 1981.

Kroehnert, Gary, *100 Training Games*, McGraw-Hill Book Company, Sydney, 1994.

Rohnke, Karl, *High Profile*, Project Adventure, Massachusetts, 1981.

Rohnke, Karl, *Silver Bullets*, Kendall Hunt Publishing, Iowa, 1984.

Rohnke, Karl, *Cowstalis and Cobras II*, Kendall Hunt Publishing, Iowa, 1989.

Orlick, Terry, *The Cooperative Sports and Games Book*, Pantheon Books, New York, 1978.

Orlick, Terry, *The Second Cooperative Sports and Games Book*, Pantheon Books, New York, 1982.

CHAPTER 27

Getting ready

Checklists are a handy tool for even the most experienced trainer

This chapter will give you a number of checklists that may be appropriate for you as a trainer. Most of the material being presented in this chapter is a summary of information that has already been presented in previous chapters. However, there are so many things that a new trainer has to learn from experience that it is impossible to tie everything up in a neat little parcel.

I would like to think that this book has assisted the new trainer in a number of ways, with these checklists adding to the support.

When you are given the task of completely organizing a new training course, you will find that there are numerous jobs that have to be done. The following checklist has been compiled to make this task easier for you.

As with all of the material in this book the checklist has been designed to suit my needs; please treat it us a base to build your own checklists.

```
┌─────────────────────────────────────────────────────────┐
│ OUTSIDE WORKSHOP CHECKLIST                               │
├─────────────────────────────────────────────────────────┤
│ COURSE TITLE: _____ │
│ COURSE DATES: _____ │
├─────────────────────────────────────────────────────────┤
│ Number of participants                                  │
│ Book venue                                              │
│ Request nominations                                     │
│ Invite speakers                                         │
│ Design topic list                                       │
│ Prepare session notes                                   │
│ Design programme                                        │
│ Write fact sheet                                        │
│ Book/order equipment                                    │
│ Book/order materials                                    │
│ Prepare handouts                                        │
│ Handouts printed                                        │
│ Prepare training aids                                   │
│ Prepare certificates                                    │
│ Book transport (speakers)                               │
│ Book transport (participants)                           │
│ Check nominations                                       │
│ Book accommodation                                      │
│ Advise supervisors                                      │
│ Confirm speakers                                        │
│ Confirm participants                                    │
│ Distribute fact sheet                                   │
│ Distribute pre-course materials                         │
│ Organise participants' needs                            │
│ Confirm accommodation                                   │
│ Purchase consumable items                               │
│ Organise coffee/tea, etc.                               │
│ Organise meals                                          │
│ Invitations to management                               │
│ Pick up films, videos, etc.                             │
│ Prepare name tags                                       │
│ Check stationery                                        │
│ Other _____                                   │
│ Other _____                                   │
│ Other _____                                   │
│ Other _____                                   │
│ Double check everything again                           │
└─────────────────────────────────────────────────────────┘
```

With so many items to check off it can become confusing to work out when certain things need to be done. You may find that this checklist is better if it's displayed in chart form as a task timeline. By transfering the information from your checklist to a task timeline you will avoid missing items.

Some of the items have been included from the previous checklist, for the example below of a task timeline.

There are computer programs available to help you organize your course diary. A critical path analysis can be worked out by entering the start date of the course and the date you want to start organizing for it. The rest of the information is worked out for you by the program. As these are complete packages I don't feel that I need to give you any other information on them.

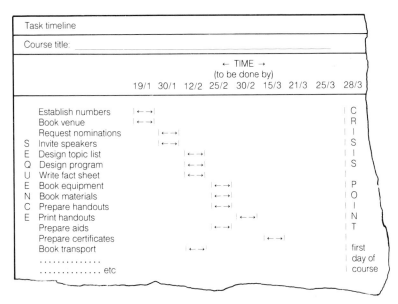

A task timeline helps you to prepare in an organized way to meet a deadline

That takes care of the course prework. Now let's look at a checklist that will be of use to new trainers who think they are ready to present a session to a group.

SESSION CHECKLIST

SESSION TITLE: _____

SESSION DATES: _____

Are your session notes legible?	_____
Are your session objectives clear?	_____
Do you know who the group is?	_____
Do you have a motivator for the group?	_____
Are you building on previous knowledge?	_____
Is the session content the right size?	_____
Do you have the right number of points?	_____
Is the sequence of points logical?	_____
Are the training aids relevant?	_____
Are the handouts clear?	_____
Are the training aids appropriate?	_____
Are the training aids all operational?	_____
Is there plenty of participant activity?	_____
Have you planned to link forward?	_____
Have you included a session summary?	_____
Is your session evaluation suitable?	_____
Have you rehearsed your session?	_____
How many principles used? — R?	_____
— A?	_____
— M?	_____
— P?	_____
— 2?	_____
— F?	_____
— A?	_____
— M?	_____
— E?	_____

The day before the course may also require a bit of input from you.

```
┌─────────────────────────────────────────────────────────────┐
│ THE DAY BEFORE CHECKLIST                                     │
├─────────────────────────────────────────────────────────────┤
│                                                             │
│ COURSE TITLE: _____       │
│                                                             │
│ COURSE DATES: _____       │
├─────────────────────────────────────────────────────────────┤
│ Is the training room ready?                       _____   │
│ Do you have extra markers, etc?                   _____   │
│ Is the equipment set up?                          _____   │
│ Is the seating arranged as required?              _____   │
│ Is all of your equipment ready?                   _____   │
│ Can everyone see you and the equipment?           _____   │
│ Are you still familiar with the material?         _____   │
│ Do you know where all of the spares are?          _____   │
└─────────────────────────────────────────────────────────────┘
```

Next is a simple checklist for you to use before the session is due to start.

```
┌─────────────────────────────────────────────────────────────┐
│ THE BEFORE YOU GO IN CHECKLIST                              │
├─────────────────────────────────────────────────────────────┤
│                                                             │
│ COURSE TITLE: _____       │
│                                                             │
│ COURSE DATES: _____       │
├─────────────────────────────────────────────────────────────┤
│ Get there early                                   _____   │
│ Recheck your equipment                            _____   │
│ Set up your training aids                         _____   │
│ Organize and place your notes                     _____   │
│ Warm up your voice                                _____   │
│ Mentally recall the sequence of events            _____   │
│ Breathe deeply                                    _____   │
└─────────────────────────────────────────────────────────────┘
```

Although the next checklist is titled 'after your presentation', it should be used shortly after you finish giving your session. By using it soon after the session you will be able to recall more of the points listed. Just recognising that parts of your session may have been better can almost solve the problem.

AFTER YOUR PRESENTATION CHECKLIST	
COURSE TITLE: _____	
COURSE DATES: _____	
Did you avoid speaking softly?	_____
Did you avoid mumbling?	_____
Did you avoid speaking slowly?	_____
Did you avoid speaking too fast?	_____
Did you avoid a monotone presentation?	_____
Did you avoid pacing?	_____
Did you avoid frequent coughing?	_____
Did you avoid indecision?	_____
Did you avoid fiddling?	_____
Did you avoid other nervous habits?	_____
Did you avoid talking to the board?	_____
Were you well prepared?	_____
Were you animated?	_____
Were you enthusiastic?	_____
Did you summarise frequently?	_____
Was there three-way communication?	_____
Was your appearance suitable?	_____
Did you use all of the nine principles?	_____
Did your audience achieve the objectives?	_____

This checklist will show you quickly whether or not your questioning techniques need to be improved.

```
┌─────────────────────────────────────────────────────────┐
│ QUESTION AND ANSWER CHECKLIST                            │
├─────────────────────────────────────────────────────────┤
│ COURSE TITLE: _____ │
│                                                         │
│ COURSE DATES: _____ │
├─────────────────────────────────────────────────────────┤
│ Do I encourage questions?                    _____  │
│ Do I anticipate the correct questions?       _____  │
│ Do I practise the correct response?          _____  │
│ Do I use eye contact to involve the group?   _____  │
│ Do I repeat the question so it is heard?      _____  │
│ Do I repeat the question for clarification?  _____  │
│ Do I listen carefully?                       _____  │
│ Do I allow other participants to answer?     _____  │
└─────────────────────────────────────────────────────────┘
```

As communication plays a major part in our training sessions, a communication checklist has been included.

```
┌─────────────────────────────────────────────────────────┐
│ COMMUNICATION CHECKLIST                                  │
├─────────────────────────────────────────────────────────┤
│ COURSE TITLE: _____ │
│                                                         │
│ COURSE DATES: _____ │
├─────────────────────────────────────────────────────────┤
│ Did I speak to the participants?             _____  │
│ Did the participants speak to me?            _____  │
│ Did the participants speak to each other?    _____  │
└─────────────────────────────────────────────────────────┘
```

If we can place three ticks on this list, we can safely say that there was a three-way communication during the training session.

It's a good idea occasionally to have someone come and sit in on your session so that you can get some constructive feedback on your teaching techniques. Make sure that you tell the observer that you are after constructive feedback, otherwise you're likely to get a blank sheet of paper given back to you.

OBSERVER'S CHECKLIST	
COURSE TITLE: _____	
COURSE DATES: _____	
Were the main points emphasised?	_____
Was eye contact made?	_____
Was eye contact kept?	_____
Did the presenter stand upright?	_____
Was the presenter's position varied enough?	_____
Was the pitch varied?	_____
Was everything clearly spoken?	_____
Did the presenter read the audience?	_____
Were the objectives achieved?	_____

Any, or all, of the other checklists may be given to an observer so that your total performance may be assessed. After all, if you don't know about it how can you fix it?

When you present a session where you feel everything went well, you will probably find that you can tick most of the points given in this checklist. Alternatively, when you give a session where you feel extremely anxious you may find that very few of these points have been taken into consideration.

NERVES CHECKLIST	
COURSE TITLE: _____	
COURSE DATES: _____	
Did you breathe deeply?	_____
Did you mentally rehearse before going in?	_____
Did you arrive early?	_____
Did you look professional?	_____
Did you try to anticipate questions?	_____
Did you check all of your equipment?	_____
Did you establish your credibility?	_____
Did you use your session notes?	_____
Did you motivate the group?	_____
Did you move around?	_____
Did you practise your presentation?	_____
Did you know what you were talking about?	_____
Did you use the self-fulfilling prophecy?	_____

Conclusion

The trainer needs to be aware of many things to prepare properly. All of these things tend to fall into one of the four categories shown below:

- trainer behavioral attitudes
- physical preparation
- mental preparation
- teaching and learning principles.

If a trainer is lacking in any of these areas, it's going to make it difficult to create a suitable learning atmosphere.

This book has attempted to cover as many of these areas as possible, but if you don't apply yourself to this information it can't work.

> THERE'S NEVER TIME
> TO DO IT PROPERLY,
> BUT THERE'S ALWAYS TIME
> TO DO IT OVER.

Further reading

As this chapter relates to the whole sphere of training and psychology, I can't create a specific list of texts for your further reading.

Just about every book that has been written about training will have some kind of input to your 'Getting Ready'. Even texts and articles that are out of date can help you. When looking at things that have been tried previously you will probably find the results of their use. It will save you experiencing the same problems.

A final word

The previous twenty-seven chapters will give you more than enough theory to allow you to become a professional trainer. However, theory alone is not enough. The time is now here for you to go and practise what has just been read.

If you are a new trainer or one with little experience, the best way to spend your time now is training and trying to improve your style. If you are fortunate enough to still have time available before you commence your first programme, use the time to study other professional trainers.

Experienced trainers who happen to be thumbing through this book will certainly be given a few new ideas and have lots of existing knowledge reinforced.

As there aren't many professional trainers in existence, I would request that those who do exist take responsibility for the coaching of the new, inexperienced or unprofessional trainers that they may come into contact with. You will find that it's an incredible buzz to see one of your trainees giving a professional performance and you know deep down that it's because of your time and their effort.

For the new trainer, happy training, and don't forget that the trainee is the most important thing for you to consider.

Common training terms

adventure training   any outdoor-based training that has a perceived high-risk factor.

adviser   someone who has the responsibility of ensuring that the trainees' learning is on the right path and is able to offer assistance when required.

aids   any form of training aid or item that assists learning or teaching.

audio-visual aids   usually an electronic training aid that has pictures and/or sound.

brainstorming   a group method for gaining lots of ideas or suggestions. Also refer to synergism.

buzz group   a small group of participants working on a task.

case study   a technique where the participants are given a situation to look at and are then required to solve problems or make decisions.

CBT   abbreviation for 'Competency-Based Training', or 'computer-based training'.

checklist   a list of relevant items either required or to be considered.

Competency-Based Training   an educational process that is based on specific competencies that have been previously identified.

computer-based training   any training that takes place on a computer and is under the direction of the program itself.

conference   a group of people who get together to exchange ideas on a specific topic.

course   refers to a group of people who are attending some form of training. It may also refer to the whole of the instruction.

DACUM   a process to develop a curriculum by breaking a job or position down into tasks.

delphi technique   a group technique for solving problems or dealing with specific situations which does not require the group to meet.

discovery learning   learners learn by doing, rather than relying heavily on the teacher.

evaluation   testing and comparing results.

exercise   refers to any structured experience in which the participants are involved.

experiential learning   the same as discovery learning.

216

facilitator a trainer who lets the group become responsible for the learning outcome. A facilitator normally controls the group process rather than just teaching.

feedback constructive information on the course material, given to the trainees or the trainer.

field trip a trip to a location to observe something to do with the training.

fishbowl a group process using a discussion group and an observer group.

flip chart an easel with large sheets of paper.

games discovery exercises where participants learn by experience. Games usually have rules and are competitive.

HRD Human Resource Development.

human resource development refers to the training or development of staff.

icebreaker a quick game or exercise designed to get participants settled or mixing with each other.

instructor the person who instructs, trains, teaches or informs an individual or a group of people.

learner-centred training a training situation where participants take responsibility for their learning.

learning contract a contract designed and followed by the learner to achieve stated objectives.

lecture a one-way communication from the lecturer to the group.

lesson see **session**.

multicultural mixed races, nationalities or cultures.

networking getting to know other participants. May be used to support or assist each other during or after the instruction.

nominal group process a structured problem-solving process that initially does not require participants to interact.

objective a statement giving the goals to be achieved.

observer someone who watches a group process and gives feedback on it.

OD organizational development.

OHP overhead projector.

OHT overhead transparency.

organizational development planned training or development of staff to meet planned organizational goals.

outdoor training training or activity that takes place outdoors.

overhead projector electronic projector that projects overhead transparency images onto a wall or screen.

overhead transparency   sheet of transparent film with information written or drawn on it. Used with overhead projectors.

participant   a person attending a training program or involved in any group process.

piloting   testing something before sending it to the target population. Questionnaires and examinations are normally piloted before they are used.

pre-work   anything the participant has to do as advance work for a course.

program   see **course**.

Recognition of Prior Learning   giving credit for previously gained knowledge or skills. This prior learning may be done either formally or informally.

recorder   the person given the task of writing down key points or ideas generated by a group.

reinforcement   encouragement or praise given to participants to keep their interest or increase their motivation.

role-play   an acting out of a specific situation in front of, or with, the group.

RPL   Recognition of Prior Learning.

seminar   an information or problem-solving session where the participants have the same need or problem identified.

session   any single presentation that deals with one specific topic. It may last from a few minutes to several days.

simulation   an exercise designed to create a real-life atmosphere.

student   see **participant**.

synergy   when a group of people get together to generate ideas, they generate more (and better) ideas than the total of the ideas that may have been generated individually.

T-group   an unstructured program where individuals find out how their behaviour affects others and vice versa.

team building   a training program designed to assist a group of people to work together as a team.

test   a way of determining a participant's level of knowledge, skill, expertise or behavior in a given area.

TNA   training needs analysis.

trainer   the person who trains, instructs, teaches or informs an individual or a group of people

training gap   see **training need**.

training need   the difference between what an employee can do now and what they are required to do in order to carry out their job effectively and efficiently.

training needs analysis   the method of determining a training need.

video   can be used to describe a video camera and recorder, a video player or a video cassette tape.

workshop   a participative training program where the participants learn by doing.

Bibliography

The body of literature in human relations training and its closely related fields is growing rapidly. The trainer who wishes to advance in this area is urged to study the concepts of training and development to their limit. This book is the starting point, and this bibliography is the next step.

The publications that have been marked with an * should be in all trainers' permanent libraries as you will find that you will be refering to them constantly.

Action Magazine, April 1992.

Ashworth, P.D. & Saxton, J., *On Competence*, 1990.

Ayers, Keith, 'Executives in the Wilderness', *Staff Recruitment, Training & Development*, 1990, 34–7.

Baird, L., Schneier, C. & Laird, D., *The Training and Development Sourcebook*, Human Resource Press, Massachusetts, 1985. *

Blanchard, Kenneth & Johnson, Spencer, *The One Minute Manager*, William Collins, Great Britain, 1983. *

Bourner, Tom, Martin, Vivien & Race, Phil, *Workshops That Work*, McGraw-Hill Book Company, London, 1993.

Boydell, T. H., *A Guide to the Identification of Training Needs*, 2nd edn, British Association for the Commercial and Industrial Education, London, 1983.

Brown, J., Lewis, R. & Harcleroad, F., *AV Instruction Technology, Media and Methods*, 6th edn, McGraw-Hill Book Company, New York, 1983.

Buller, Paul, Cragun, John & McEvoy, Glenn, 'Getting the Most out of Outdoor Training', *Training & Development Journal*, March 1991, 45 (3), 58–61.

Christopher, Elizabeth & Smith, Larry, *Leadership Training through Gaming*, Nichols Publishing Company, New York, 1987.

Cohen, L. & Manion, L., *Research Methods in Education*, Croom Helm, London, 1980.

Collard, Mark & Thompson, Bill, 'Adventure Approach to Corporate Training', *Training and Development in Australia*, March 1992, 19 (1), 11–13.

Collins, Roger & Saul, Peter, *Management Competencies Development Program*, McGraw-Hill Book Company, Sydney, 1991.

Confederation of Australian Industry, *CBT: Proposals For the Australian Vocational Educational and Training System*, 1991.

Craig, Robert, *Training and Development Handbook*, 2nd edn, McGraw-Hill Book Company, New York, 1976. *

Dale, Edgar, *Audiovisual Methods in Teaching*, 3rd edn, The Dryden Press, Illinois, 1969.

Daniels, William, *Group Power: A Manager's Guide to Using Meetings*, University Associates, California, 1986.

Dimock, Hedley, *Groups: Leadership and Group Development*, University Associates, California, 1987.

Donaldson, Les & Scannell, Edward, *Human Resource Development: The New Trainer's Guide*, 2nd edn, Addison-Wesley Publishing Company, Massachusetts, 1986.

Dowling, J. R. & Drolet, R. P., *Developing and Administering an Industrial Training Program*, CBI Publishing, Massachusetts, 1979.

Earl, Tony, *The Art and Craft of Course Design*, Nichols Publishing, New York, 1987.

Easterby-Smith, Mark, *Evaluation of Management Education, Training and Development*, Gower Publishing Company, England, 1986.

Eitington, Julius, *The Winning Trainer*, Gulf Publishing Company, Houston, 1984. *

Elgood, Chris, *Handbook of Management Games*, 4th edn, Gower Publishing Company, England, 1988.

Field, Laurie, *Skilling Australia*, Longman Cheshire, Melbourne, 1990. *

Field, Laurie, *Teaching Practical Work at TAFE*, Published by ITATE, Sydney, 1984.

Fluegelman, Andrew, *The New Games Book*, Doubleday, New York, 1976.

Fluegelman, Andrew, *More New Games*, Doubleday, New York, 1981.

Forbess-Greene, Sue, *The Encyclopedia of Icebreakers*, University Associates, California, 1983.

Foyster, John, *Getting To Grips With Competency Based Training and Assessment*, TAFE, South Australia. 1990.

Galagan, Patricia, 'Between Two Trapezes', *Training & Development Journal*, March 1987, 41 (3), 40–8.

Gall, Adrienne, 'You Can Take the Managers out of the Woods, but . . .' *Training & Development Journal*, March 1987, 41 (3), 54–8.

Gibbs, Graham, Habeshaw, Sue & Habeshaw, Trevor, *53 Interesting Things To Do in Your Lectures*, 2nd edn, Whitehall Printing Company, England, 1987.

Goad, Tom, *Delivering Effective Training*, University Associates, California, 1982.

Goldstein, Irwin, *Training: Program Development and Evaluation*, Brooks/ Cole Publishing, California, 1974.

Gronlund, Norman, *Stating Objectives for Classroom Instruction*, 3rd edn, Macmillan Publishing, New York, 1985.

Hager, P., Gonzi, A. & Oliver, L., *Competency Based Approaches to Professional Education*, 1990.

Hamblin, A. C., *Evaluation and Control of Training*, McGraw-Hill Book Company, London, 1974.

Hanson, Philip, *Learning through Groups: A Trainer's Basic Guide*, University Associates, California, 1981.

Henerson, Marlene, *How To Measure Attitudes*, Sage Publications, California, 1987.

Howes, Virgil, *Individualisation of Instruction*, Macmillan Publishing, New York, 1970.

Huszczo, Gregory, 'Training for Team Building', *Training & Development Journal*, February 1990, 44 (2), 37–43.

Jones, Ken, *Imaginative Events for Training*, McGraw-Hill Book Company, New York, 1993.

Kirkpatrick, Donald, *Supervisory Training and Development*, 2nd edn, Addison-Wesley Publishing Company, Massachusetts, 1983.

Klemp, G. O., *Job Competence Assessment: Defining the Attributes of the Top Performer*, 1982.

Knowles, Malcolm, *Self-Directed Learning*, Cambridge, New York, 1975.

Knowles, Malcolm, *The Adult Learner: A Neglected Species*, 2nd edn, Gulf Publishing Company, Houston, 1978. *

Knowles, Malcolm, *Using Learning Contracts*, Jossey-Bass Publishers, California, 1986.

Kroehnert, Gary, *100 Training Games*, McGraw-Hill Book Company, Sydney, 1994. *

Laird, Dugan, *Approaches to Training and Development*, Addison-Wesley Publishing Company, Massachusetts, 1978. *

Long, Janet, 'The Wilderness Lab Comes of Age', *Training & Development Journal*, March 1987, 41 (3), 30–9.

McDonald, S., *Competency-Based Training Pilot Projects Data Base*, Vocational Educational, Employment and Training Advisory Committee (VEETAC), 1991.

Mager, Robert, *Developing Attitudes toward Learning*, 2nd edn, David S. Lake Publishers, California, 1984.

Mager, Robert, *Measuring Instructional Results*, 2nd edn, Pitman Learning Company, California, 1984.

Mager, Robert, *Preparing Instructional Objectives*, 2nd edn, Pitman Learning Company, California, 1984. *

Mager, Robert & Pipe, Peter, *Analysing Performance Problems*, 2nd edn, David S. Lake Publishers, California, 1984.

Mill, Cyril, *Activities for Trainers: 50 Useful Designs*, University Associates California, 1980.

Minor, E., *Handbook for Preparing Visual Media*, 2nd edn, McGraw-Hill Book Company, New York, 1978.

Minor, E. & Frye, H., *Techniques for Producing Visual Instructional Media*, McGraw-Hill Book Company, New York, 1970.

Morris, Kenneth & Cinnamon, Kenneth, *A Handbook of Non-verbal Group Exercises*, Applied Skills Press, California, 1983.

Morris, Kenneth & Cinnamon, Kenneth, *A Handbook of Verbal Group Exercises*, Applied Skills Press, California, 1983.

National Competency Standards, Department of Employment, Education and Training (DEET), 1991.

Newstrom, J. W. & Scannell, E. E., *Games Trainers Play*, McGraw-Hill Book Company, New York, 1980.

Newstrom, J. W., & Scannell, E. E., *Still More Games Trainers Play*, McGraw-Hill Book Company, New York, 1991.

Newstrom, J. W., & Scannell, E. E., *Even More Games Trainers Play*, McGraw-Hill Book Company, New York, 1994.

Nilson, Carolyn, *Team Games for Trainers*, McGraw-Hill Book Company, New York, 1993.

Orlick, Terry, *The Cooperative Sports and Games Book*, Pantheon Books, New York, 1978.

Orlick, Terry, *The Second Cooperative Sports and Games Book*, Pantheon Books, New York, 1982.

Owens, Robert, *Organisational Behaviour in Education*, 3rd edn, Prentice-Hall International, New Jersey, 1987.

Pagano, Robert, *Understanding Statistics in the Behavioral Sciences*, West Publishing, Minnesota, 1981.

Pease, Allan, *Body Language*, Camel Publishing Company, North Sydney, 1981.

Pennington, F. C., *Assessing Educational Needs of Adults*, New Directions for Continuing Education Quarterly Sourcebooks, Jossey-Bass, San Francisco, 1980, Series No. 7.

Poulter, Bruce, *Training and Development*, CCH Australia Limited, Australia, 1982.

Rae, Leslie, *How to Measure Training Effectiveness*, Gower Publishing Company, England, 1987.

Reeves, T. & Harper, D., *Surveys at Work*, McGraw-Hill Book Company, London, 1981.

Rogers, Jennifer, *Adults Learning*, 2nd edn, Open University Press, England, 1979.

Rohnke, Karl, *High Profile*, Project Adventure, Massachusetts, 1981.

Rohnke, Karl, *Silver Bullets*, Kendall Hunt Publishing, Iowa, 1984.

Rohnke, Karl, *Cowstalis and Cobras II*, Kendall Hunt Publishing, Iowa, 1989.

Rumsey, D. J. & Hawke, G. A., *Competency-Based Testing—A TAFE Approach,* TAFE, 1988.

Scannell, E. E. & Newstrom, J. W., *More Games Trainers Play*, McGraw-Hill Book Company, New York, 1983.

Stammers, R. & Patrick, J., *The Psychology of Training*, Methuen & Company, London, 1975.

TAFE, *Assessing Competency in the Workplace*, Open College Network, Sydney, 1990.

Tindall, K., Collins, B. & Reid, D., *The Electronic Classroom*, McGraw-Hill Book Company, Sydney, 1973.

Thompson, Brad Lee, 'Training in the Great Outdoors', *Training*, May 1991, 28 (5), 46–52.

Van Ments, Morry, *The Effective Use of Role-Play*, Kogan Page Limited, London, 1987.

Video, *You'll Soon Get The Hang Of It*, Video Arts. *

Video, *Right First Time*, NSW TAFE.

Wagner, Richard, Baldwin, Timothy & Roland, Christopher, 'Outdoor Training: Revolution or Fad?', *Training & Development Journal*, March 1991, 45 (3), 51–7.

Wilson, Larry, 'Come to the Ranch and Play the Game', *Training & Development Journal*, March 1987, 41 (3), 49–50.

Zemke, R. & Kramlinger, T., *Figuring Things Out: A Trainer's Guide to Needs and Task Analysis*, Addison-Wesley Publishing Company, Massachusetts, 1981.

Zenger, John, Musselwhite, Ed, Hurson, Kathleen & Perrin, Craig, 'Leadership in a Team Environment', *Training & Development*, October 1991, 45 (10), 47–52.

Index

In-House Training Services

If you would like information on our In-house training services please complete the information below and forward it on to us by mail.

Name: _____

Title: _____

Organization: _____

Address: _____

_____

_____

Phone: _____

Fax: _____

I would like further information on:
In-house Training Techniques courses
In-house courses for other subjects

_____

_____

_____

_____

_____

_____

Post to: Gary Kroehnert
         Training Excellence Pty Limited
         PO Box 71
         Grose Vale NSW 2753
         Australia

Readers' comments and suggestions

If you would like to comment on any of the things written (or not written) about in this book, now is your time to do it. I would also appreciate suggestions and comments on the layout, wording or anything else you feel needs comment.

Gary Kroehnert

Suggestions for improvements

_____

_____

_____

_____

_____

_____

Additional comments

_____

_____

_____

_____

_____

_____

Please cut this form out and return it to the Publisher, Business and Professional, McGraw-Hill Book Company Australia Pty Limited.